Hunting Bears

Black, Brown, Grizzly, and Polar Bears

Hunting Bears

Black, Brown, Grizzly, and Polar Bears

Kathy Etling

DEDICATION

To my husband, Bob, who supported me in numerous ways during the writing of this
book. I would also like to dedicate this book to all the wonderful animals
I have had the privilege to hunt, to spot, and to take, including those that were much
too crafty for me, and thus were able to get away and, I hope, provided
a special memory for yet another lucky hunter.

Front cover image: Bob Beaulieu
Page ii image: Bob Fromme
Back cover images: Jim Zumbo and Canada North Outfitting
Score chart for bear reprinted courtesy of the Boone and Crockett Club,
250 Station Dr., Missoula, MT 59801
(406)542-1888, www.boone-crockett.org.

Published by: Woods N' Water, Inc.
Peter and Kate Fiduccia
P.O. Box 65
Bellvale, NY 10912

Printed in the United States of America
10 9 8 7 6 5 4 3 2 1
ISBN: 0-9722804-1-3

TABLE OF CONTENTS

THE MOST DANGEROUS GAME!

Many years ago a writer far more talented than I put pen to paper and composed an outstanding short story called "The Most Dangerous Game." In this short story, a big game hunter has become bored with all of the world's great wildlife species. We know this because the story's hero is taken inside the hunter's lodge while the hunter explains the circumstances surrounding each of the animal trophies he has taken.

The twist in this story is that the hero himself has been brought to the hunter's island haunt to become the hunter's latest prey. The hero is the most dangerous game, according to the hunter, because he can think and plan and strike back and, perhaps, even gain the upper hand and win this most dangerous game.

I will not ruin the story for you, because it remains a notable piece of fine literature and one worth reading even if you read it many years ago and don't remember how it ended—not that I can imagine anyone forgetting. I know I never will.

That is how good literature should affect you. While I do not pretend that this book is in any way, shape, or form, good literature, I do hope that it is both educational and thought-provoking for would-be and current bear hunters.

Bears, like humans, are considered highly intelligent, fierce when provoked, able to wreak revenge if the mood hits them, and dangerous. While humans have the upper hand in most cases, the bear can be quick to gain advantage. It is this element of risk and surprise that holds us in awe of them. It is the very notion of going up against an animal that is our equal in some ways and very much our superior in others that drives us as we save our money, sight in our guns, and test our bows—and then leave the warmth and safety of our homes to meet up with this grandest—and most dangerous—of creatures on its own turf.

Yes, bears are dangerous. We admire and respect them, as did our forefathers , for those very traits. And yet these huge animals, some with five-inch-long claws at the tips of roasting-pan-size paws, more often than not choose to run from an encounter with us.

Through the ages, we as a species have whittled away at the bear's supremacy until today perhaps even bears are no longer aware of how powerful and strong and magnificent they still are.

Today we hold the fate of all the world's bear species in our hands. We can save these threatened and endangered animals or allow their numbers to dwindle and them to disappear from the earth.

For in our drive to populate every bit of wilderness, extract the last drop of oil from the earth, and constantly push bears into habitats that can no longer support them, all for the gratification of recently acquired habits, it is truly we humans who are now the most dangerous game. Not for our intellect and reason, so cherished by that long-ago writer of fiction, but for our tendency to focus only on ourselves and our desires, to the detriment of any other living species that get in the way.

Like the bears.

—*Kathy Etling*

ACKNOWLEDGEMENTS

The writing of any book about the biology, behaviors, history, and hunting of bears is never a solo or totally independent project. I absolutely would have been unable to do this book on my own, that is the plain and simple truth.

Although I long have been fascinated by bears, cougars, and other large predators, I have never hunted them. I have hunted other creatures who share the woods with bears on numerous occasions, and I also have observed and interacted with bears during many of my trips to the West, while both hunting and hiking. Through many years of casual and serious study I have gained a tremendous respect for both these animals and for the people who hunt them, many of whom have been of inestimable help as I have pieced this book together.

First, I would like to thank my good friend and mentor, Jim Zumbo, hunting editor of Outdoor Life, for his advice, time, and anecdotes as well as the generous loan of his entire library of bear and bear hunting photos and slides. Jim has hunted bears for many years. His insights were truly of inestimable value.

I would also like to thank M. R. James, editor emeritus of Bowhunter Magazine, another dear friend who has also come to my aid on many previous occasions. M. R. is a guru of black bear hunting, as you will soon see for yourself while reading this book. M. R. has bowhunted black bears in many different states and provinces. He has taken ordinary black bears and huge, trophy bears, and he has done so while using a variety of different strategies and tactics. M. R. actually enjoys getting "up close and personal" with black bears, whether he chooses to harvest one or not. It shows in the wealth of anecdotes, hunting advice, and photos he has so graciously shared with us.

Although I have never met Jerome Knap, owner-outfitter of Canada North Outfitting, he too went above and beyond the call of duty. Jerome not only consented to an interview, he forwarded from his office many large, full-color photos of polar bears, polar bear hunters, and polar bear hunting incidents and situations that few other people have ever before been privileged to view. These photos, like the ones from Jim Zumbo and M. R. James, are all first-rate, and put the viewer in the thick of what it must feel like to be hunting Nanuq. I feel very fortunate to have been entrusted with their use, as well as to be able to pick a brain as full of bear lore as Jerome's.

Cody, Wyoming, elk outfitter Ron Dube also helped. Ron operates Ron Dube's Wilderness Adventures, an outfit that once guided many bear hunters both spring and fall. Although Ron no longer guides bear hunters, his store of bear hunting knowledge is vast, and his recall outstanding. He too provided me with many excellent photos, lots of anecdotes, and more time than he probably had to spare.

Larry Heathington, another old friend, has forgotten more about calling black bears than most other people have ever learned. Larry's knowledge of the topic is astounding, and he is also one of the finest teachers of wildlife lore I've ever had the privilege of working with. Larry has always been generous to a fault with his time, knowledge, advice, and photos, and he came through for me once more as I worked on this project.

Missouri building contractor Warren Parker is probably best known as an ex-president of Safari Club International. Warren is a busy man and yet he graciously consented to both an interview with a writer whom he had never before met, as well as the loan of his precious bear photos. Precious, because Warren has hunted bears all over the globe. He has taken magnificent specimens of either all or most of the bears worldwide that may be legally hunted. His contributions were invaluable to this project. My dear Alaskan friend, Marlin Grasser, is also to be commended for his generosity in relating so many different bear stories to me over the years, including the one in which he was very nearly killed. Marlin, a retired Alaskan outfitter and

Master Guide, was also responsible for chasing off the grizzly bear that had its nose against my skull—with only the thin fabric of our tent between those two objects. The bear exercised a great deal of restraint in not champing down, when it knew full well that my husband had stowed his recently harvested Dall sheep's skull inside our tiny tent for "safe-keeping." I would also like to thank the many biologists with various state and federal agencies who have worked with me through the years on myriad previous bear books and bear articles. Thanks to the guidance of men like Tom Smith of the U.S. Geological Service in Alaska, Kevin Frey of Montana Fish, Wildlife & Parks, Dave Moody and Mark Bruscino of the Wyoming Game and Fish Department, Dave Hamilton of the Missouri Department of Conservation, Bill Mytton, formerly with the Wisconsin Department of Natural Resources, Gary Alt of the Pennsylvania Department of Conservation, Bill Beck, formerly with the Colorado Division of Wildlife, and Matt Austin of the British Columbia Ministry of the Environment, as well as most of the bear biologists on staff with the Alaska Department of Fish and Game. Without these men my knowledge and understanding of the various North American bears would be far less than what it is.

Thanks as well to my dear friend Madleine Kay, her husband Mike Fejes, Gloria Erickson, Phyllis Tucker, and my editor Dave Dolbee of Petersen's Bowhunting. Thanks as well to Bob Fromme.

Special thanks are in order for the prestigious Boone and Crockett Club, particularly my dear friend Jack Reneau, director of the records-keeping division, and his associate, Chris Tonkinson, for their help in providing me help at various stages during the writing of this book and also for permission to reproduce within these pages various charts and maps copyrighted by the club.

I would also like to thank Dalton Carr, the Colorado man who probably has taken more black bears than any living American, and the author of his own fine bear book, *Tales of a Bear Hunter*.

Thanks also to Bob Beaulieu, Bob McGuire, Bruce Pelletier, Hal Blood, Larry Kaniut, Mike McDonald, Chuck Schlindwein, the late Charles Wolter, and the late Terry Kayser.

Thanks too to my publisher Peter Fiduccia, whose idea it was to write this bear hunting book, his lovely wife and my copy editor, Kate Fiduccia, whose patience and forebearance was tested severely after my computer crashed not once, but twice, during the research phase of the project, losing most of my notes and interviews and delaying the manuscript's completion by a number of months.

I would also like to thank all the bear conservation groups who have commissioned the numerous bear studies now posted on the Internet for everyone to peruse. What a fantastic addition to my own personal library of bear-related materials this provided.

Finally, I would like to thank whoever invented the Internet—I don't think it was Al Gore —for providing writers everywhere with a research source more invaluable than any I can think of, particularly if said writer lives far from a major library like I do.

Without the aid of all these wonderful people—as well as the Internet—this book would not have been possible.

Thank you one and all.

THE SPIRIT BEAR

Modern humans stand alone at the top of the food chain. Few of us seem to realize or care that to attain our position as the very real "top dog" of our time, other creatures had to be displaced. The most notable of the nonhuman rulers of previous ages include, ironically, a group of animals that in many ways resemble humans. Those animals are the bears.

Our ancestors recognized in bears many human traits, and for this they both honored the animals and feared them. Scientists who have studied the primitive relationship that existed between those peoples and bears came to understand that it was unique. During a time when humans attempted to control the uncertain world around them through magic and mysticism, numerous rites were dedicated to placating bears and their spirits. Bears were big medicine. They stood erect like humans, used shelters or dens, cared for their offspring until the youngsters were old enough to fend for themselves, and left a paw print more like a human's track than that of almost any other species. A bear's eyes see much like a human's eyes do, too. They are placed in the front of the bear's skull so that the animals, like humans, have stereoscopic vision. Bears' paws are remarkable dexterous, and the animals are incredibly curious. Bears are highly intelligent and will fight to the death to defend their young, their mates, their livelihoods, or their kills.

Adding to the mystical hold bears exerted upon early people was the great physical similarity between their form and the human form. A bear standing on its hind legs looks a like a man in a shaggy coat, but even more striking, a bear's skinned carcass resembles a human body.

Our ancestors' lives were difficult. Each year, as the sun's rays grew weaker and winter visited the earth, they fasted and sacrificed to appease the spirit of the sun god, which seemed so displeased that was abandoning the earth. They had little concept of science, and the core of their beliefs was simple: A spirit lived within and ruled each entity around them. Living in harmony with these spirits was supremely important when humans' grip upon life itself was tenuous at best. Early humans surely realized that they were far less powerful than beasts like mammoths, lions, and bears. They understood that without animals and the ready source of protein and fat they represented, they, their families, and their tribes would die. Early people owed animals a tremendous debt. For that reason, Siegfried Giedion, writing in *The Eternal Present: The Beginnings of Art*, concluded that early humans believed they were intrinsically inferior to animals.

Primitive people gradually developed better weapons and more sophisticated strategies for hunting even the largest animals. As they did, they came to a new conclusion: Humans might actually be the equals of animals. With equality came the notion of brotherhood. Such an idea has today been reborn in the ranks of animal rights extremists, who believe that any animal death is one animal death too many. During a time when human life depended on animal deaths, though, the lines were black-and-white. The stakes were too high for shades of gray.

Humans relied on their brothers and sisters, the animals, for their very lives. They revered the coyote for its cunning, the deer for its fleetness of foot, and the bear for its wisdom and strength. Before long, humans formed animal "fan clubs," where shamans or medicine men would invoke animal spirits to bless human endeavors. Totemism developed, and tales honoring animals were told and passed from one generation to the next. Through the ages, perhaps no greater bond was forged than an early one linking humans and bears.

A cave in Drachenloch, Switzerland, was described by well-known author and mythologist Joseph Campbell as having been used for the "ritual of the bear." No one can know for certain that such rituals took place here, but evidence—ancient altars and bear skulls placed strategically and seemingly deliberately within the cave's hidden chambers—seems to suggest that they did.

In Regordou, France, site of a known Neanderthal campsite, a brown bear's body was buried in a trench and then covered with a large gravestone. Neanderthals eventually died out—why, no one knows. These early people may not have been equipped with the skills to compete for existence with modern humanity's more direct human ancestors, yet they shared with them a reverence for the bear.

Deep within a Bavarian cave during the early twentieth century, explorers discovered ten large bear skulls stacked high atop a platform, apparently the work of yet another band of primitive humans. Why else would these early people have gone to great trouble laboring within the bowels of the earth but to honor the spirit of their brother, the bear?

Many of us modern humans probably owe our very existence to an ancestor who made it through a brutal winter by huddling in a bearskin or subsisting during a famine on bear meat and fat. The surnames *Bear, Baer, Brown* and *Bruner* owe their etymologies to these great beasts.

Look at other words in every modern language to see the bear's direct influence upon our culture. The Greek word for bear is *arctos,* and from this we arrive at *Arctic,* a region where the greatest of bears still thrive today. *Arctos* is also the root of *Arthur,* England's legendary king, rumored to be sleeping (like a hibernating bear) on the island of Avalon. *Bern,* Switzerland, and *Berlin,* Germany, are both named for bears.

Barley is the bear's grain because early humans fermented it underground to make beer, another word derived from *bear.* The bodies of our human dead are often placed upon *biers* in the hope that they, like the dormant bear, will one day be resurrected.

The ancient Inuit believed that polar bears remove their coats to become human when entering Inuit homes, and that upon leaving they assume their true bear shapes again. Bears are said to have taught tribes to dance and sing as well as to find healing plants. The medicinal powers found in bearberry, bear clover, bear grass, and bearwood were the gifts of our brother, the bear.

The constellation Boötes, the Bear Keeper or Bear Hunter, remains forever at the heels of Ursa Major and Ursa Minor. The name of the brightest star in Boötes, Arcturus, is derived from two Greek words: *arctos* for bear, and *ouros* for keeper.

By the time humans discovered art, they probably believed that everything in the natural world possessed a soul, including themselves and animals—including most certainly bears, for bears were big medicine indeed. Cave painting began—no one knows for certain why—in the latter half of the last ice age.

What is very telling about these paintings is not what they depict, but what they don't depict. Many species are represented, but there are only a few bears. Forty thousand years ago, a mere eyeblink in evolutionary time, humankind may have considered the spirit of the bear too powerful to trifle with, even by its little brothers and sisters.

Another age would soon dawn–our own Modern Age–during which humans now reigned supreme, many with little regard for some of the creatures without which human life might have ceased to exist. Included in this group were many of the bears, animals formerly honored when people were fearful of them, but persecuted and, in many cases, nearly driven to extinction once the roles were reversed.

When the minds of modern-day developers and magnates begin to cloud over with hubris, let us hope that something of the same awe and reverence our ancestors felt seeps through to their own inner bear spirits. For in saving the bear and its last wild places, an important part of what made us who we are will be saved as well.

—*Kathy Etling*

ALL ABOUT BEARS

There is great order in nature. Humankind has long suspected as much, even before people possessed the wherewithal to investigate the topic further. In the fourth century before the birth of Christ, Aristotle, who worked with animals, and Theophrastus, who was devoted to the study of plants, tried to classify the items in their collections. Alexander the Great, a pupil of Aristotle, aided his former teacher in this quest by sending back to Aristotle any new varieties of animals he found in foreign lands. Aristotle first attempted to classify animals based on their native habitats. He later established eight major animal groups, four he believed to have blood and the other four he thought to be bloodless. Believe it or not, Aristotle's system was used until the eighteenth century, when a Swedish botanist, Carl von Linné, refined into a workable scheme all of the best features of preceding classification attempts. The Linnaean system can expand and adjust to include not only known organisms, but also those not yet discovered. This system also gives scientists the flexibility to reclassify organisms should new findings warrant it.

CLASSIFICATION

The Linnaean system categorizes bears in the kingdom *Animalia,* phylum *Chordata,* class *Mammalia,* order *Carnivora,* suborder *Fissipedia,* superfamily *Arctoidea,* and family *Ursidae.* What these Latin terms mean is simply this: bears are warm-blooded animals equipped to eat meat. They possess spinal cords, and females of the species nurse their young with milk produced by mammary glands. Bears are also subclassified because they possess distinctly separated toes.

ORIGINS

Bears originated and evolved in North America. A "reverse migration" across Beringia, the land bridge that once connected North America to Russia, resulted the eventual population of most of Asia and Europe by bears. Bears now inhabit every continent except Africa, Antarctica, and Australia. There are eight species inhabiting parts of Asia, Europe, North America, and South America. Asian species include the giant panda *(Ailuropoda melanoleuca)* of China, the sun bear *(Helarctos malayanus)* of the Asian tropics, the sloth bear *(Melursus ursinus)* of eastern India and neighboring countries, and the Asiatic black bear *(Ursus thibetanus).*

The spectacled bear *(Tremarctos ornatus)* inhabits the Andean region of South America. Three bear species inhabit the North American continent: *Ursus americanus,* the American black bear; *Ursus arctos,* the brown or grizzly bear; and *Ursus maritimus,* the polar bear. The American black bear is native only to North America, while the range of the brown bear extends across portions of North America, Eurasia, Japan, and western Europe. The polar bear inhabits the northernmost regions of Eurasia and North America.

Bears can live in many habitats, from the high Arctic to the tropics, grasslands, and forests. They can even eke out an existence on the tundra or in the desert, although they avoid sandy desert regions.

In 1918, C. H. Merriam identified a mind-boggling eighty-six species of grizzlies and brown bears in North America alone. Today, however, only one species of brown bear is recognized worldwide, *Ursus arctos.* Some scientists further identify North America's two main brown bear species by using the subspecies names of *Ursus arctos middendorfii* for the Alaska brown bear, and *Ursus arctos horribilis* for the grizzly.

The brown bear's worldwide range extends from Spain's Cantabrian Mountains across the breadth of Russia, into Alaska, down through western Canada, and into northern and western portions of the United States. Brown bears inhabit thirty-eight countries, far more than any other bear species.

FOOD AND EATING HABITS

Bears belong to the order *Carnivora,* a grouping of land mammals that possess predators' teeth. The jaws of most mammals in this order are equipped top and bottom with *carnassial* teeth—teeth adapted specifically for tearing meat and shearing it from the bone.

Despite bears' inclusion in *Carnivora,* however, their jaws have evolved to the point that they no longer possess carnassials, although they still have canine teeth and incisors, both of which are useful for killing prey and tearing flesh. Every bear species except the polar bear is omnivorous—they'll eat just about anything—but most of the time they prefer plant matter. (This fact may shock those harboring notions of bears as bloodthirsty animals!)

Bears are generalists when it comes to obtaining their food. They are predators—strong, fast, and possessed of formidable weapons—yet both brown and black bears probably kill other animals far less frequently than might be supposed.

SIMILARITY TO OTHER ANIMALS

Bears are closely related to dogs, raccoons, and weasels. The oldest species of bear, as determined by molecular analyses, is the extremely endangered giant panda. Fossil records reveal that an ancestral giant panda existed about eighteen million years ago.

BEARS OF NORTH AMERICA

Alaska is unique among the states and provinces of North America in that all three North American bears flourish there. Although scientists don't distinguish between brown and grizzly bears, ordinary people believe there is a definite difference, and even the scientists classify them into separate subspecies. Sure, the brown is larger than the grizzly, and the Kodiak brown is on average the largest North American bear of all. But as I wrote earlier, to scientists, a Kodiak brown bear is an Alaska brown bear is a grizzly bear. Because winters are often less severe along the coastlines where

The bear's close relationship to the raccoon is clearly obvious in this photo. (Courtesy: Jim Zumbo)

Kodiak and Alaska brown bears live, and spring comes sooner and winter arrives later and, most importantly, salmon provide these coastal browns with a ready supply of high-quality protein, they're usually larger than grizzlies.

Brown/grizzly bears range over many of the islands of southeastern Alaska to the west and north well above the Arctic Circle. Black bears inhabit most of Alaska's timberlands. Polar bears, a species that evolved from the brown bear and remains an extremely close relative, roam over pack ice, ice floes, and the tundra of extreme northern and western Alaska.

HUMANLIKE ATTRIBUTES

Bears are large, heavy-bodied animals with powerfully built limbs. They are the largest of all carnivores. Bears are *plantigrade,* as humans are—they walk on the soles of their feet with their heels touching the ground. Bears can also stand up on their hind legs for extended periods of time and sit as humans do. When bears walk, their front feet turn inward, making them appear slightly pigeon-toed. Unlike humans, however, the bear's big toe is on the outside of its foot, an adaptation that probably helps these large animals to maintain balance when standing erect.

Each paw, or foot, is tipped with five long, curving claws that are longer in the springtime, after hibernation, since bears do not grub or dig while denned up. Of all the bears, brown bears have the most formidable claws.

With their remarkably dexterous prehensile paws, bears can open lids, door latches, trash cans, and freezers. Strong evidence suggests that polar bears sometimes kill seals using rocks or chunks of ice. Such behaviors approach those of the

3

African primates and serve to challenge formerly held opinions regarding the relative intelligence of disparate animal species.

Bears have large, rounded heads with small eyes. Stereoscopic vision allows them to focus keenly on an object, almost to the exclusion of all else. A bear's peripheral vision probably is no better than that of a human, unlike that of prey animals whose eyes are set on the sides of their heads to provide them with great visual

Salmon provide coastal brown bears with a ready supply of high-quality protein that these animals can feed on without expending much effort. (Courtesy: Jim Zumbo)

acuity laterally and toward the rear. Research has proven that bears can see color.

Bears, particularly those that inhabit northern regions, grow long, beautiful coats of hair. Most bears have few markings, although individuals of some species will sometimes sport either a cream-colored or white throat or chest patch which is known as a blaze. South America's spectacled bear, with its ornate 'spectacle' markings around its eyes and face, is not only smaller it is also more colorful than most other bear species. China's giant panda, however, with its distinctive black and white pelt, remains the flashiest–and most recognizable–of all the bears.

All bears are curious, intelligent, and potentially dangerous. Contrary to popular belief, although bears can see almost as well as humans, they rely more on their noses than either their eyes or ears.

BEHAVIOR

Most bears tend to avoid people. Usually, if you give a bear the opportunity to do the right thing (stay away from you), it will. Each year millions of people recreate in prime bear habitat, but surprisingly few people even see the animals. Although many of these folks don't take the proper precautions, bears almost always prefer to give humans a wide berth rather than stir up trouble, which is fortunate considering their huge physical advantage over us.

Undisturbed bears move about freely both day and night, but heavy human activity can make them shy and secretive. When hunting pressure or human activity interferes with daily bear business, most of their movement occurs at dusk or during early morning hours.

A bear's home range will be the size it needs to be. Bears are not averse to travel, are excellent swimmers, and will cover as much territory as they must to find life's necessities: food, water, and cover, including a winter den. Where food is abundant and cover dense, bears become real homebodies. Where food is scattered, the size of a bear's home range increases. During the breeding season, boars of all species range over their entire territories in search of estrous sows.

For most of their lifetimes bears are relatively solitary animals with no long-lasting bonds, but there are obvious exceptions. Cubs and mother bears remain together anywhere from one and one-half to four years, and boars and estrous sows seek each other out during the breeding season. Bears are occasionally found in great concentrations in areas where food is plentiful, such as salmon streams, berry patches, and carrion sites.

Bears go on true feeding binges late each summer and into autumn. This *hyperphagia* is probably stimulated by decreasing amounts of light, which sets into

Cubs and mother bears remain together from one and one-half to four years. (Courtesy: Jim Zumbo)

motion a complicated series of interrelated physiological signals that culminates when bears begin consuming vast quantities of food in order to put on enough weight to survive their dormancy periods. Females, especially, need to pack on the pounds, for not only will they be in gestation, but they will also give birth to cubs, and then must provide milk for those cubs until the family leaves the den later the next spring.

Animals as big and powerful as bears are capable of harming and killing each other. Although rare, dominant males will fight usurpers to the death over a female in estrus, while a female, if given the opportunity, will kill any male attempting to harm her young. Bears will also fight to protect their food, particularly a kill that was taken only after a difficult fight, or during periods when prey animals are scarce. Because bears can be so dangerous to others of their species, a pecking order or hierarchical structure is a biological necessity. Without a heirarchical structure in which every individual bear is well aware of his or her place on the social scale, bear society would be extremely chaotic and in constant turmoil.

MATING HABITS

When bears mate, the pair stays together for only a few days. During this time, they copulate repeatedly, because the female bear is an induced ovulator. In other words, female bears must be stimulated several times to start ovulation. Like other mammals in the order *Carnivora,* the male bear has a bony structure in his penis called a *baculum* and which, in older males, can attain a length of five inches or more. It is the structure that stimulates ovulation in the female bear. The baculum also locks the two bears together as they copulate. The breeding pair remains connected in a *copulatory* tie anywhere from ten to thirty minutes. Male bears will mate with every estrous female they encounter. A female will mate with male bears until the end of their estrous period.

Even though young male bears of all species are fertile and capable of breeding at three or four years of age, they rarely get the opportunity to do so in the wild. In most bear populations there is intense male competition for estrous females, and the biggest, most dominant bears do the majority of the breeding. In Alaskan brown bears, for example, males do not reach their maximum size until they are eight to ten years of age. So even after a male brown bear attains sexual maturity at age three or four, it usually must grow several more years to become a serious breeding contender. Any young male displaying amorous intent with an estrous female usually will be chased away quickly by larger, more mature males.

A female bear's fertilized eggs—*blastocysts*—do not implant in her uterus until up to five months after conception. During the time between conception and implantation, the blastocysts float within the sow's uterus. Scientists believe that the blastocysts are implanted in the uterine wall later in the year so that the young will be born at the time it is easiest for their mother to care for them—while she is denned up for the winter. A litter usually consists of one or two cubs, although sometimes up to four are born. Cubs are born small, helpless, and hairless. Their eyes are shut. They crawl about on their dormant mother to suckle her rich milk, and they increase in size until the family leaves the den later in the spring.

Contrary to what is depicted in *The Bear,* a popular movie, boars do not return to help sows raise their young, nor do bears mate for life. A male and female remain together for at most a few hours or days during the mating season. When a male leaves a female, he immediately starts searching for another receptive sow and will try to mate with as many sows as possible each year of his life. The breeding season is the only time of year when male bears will fight each other for female companionship.

If a male *does* return to a female, it will be to attempt to kill her cubs, not to mate, since she will become sexually receptive again only after her cubs are gone. This is why females with young are more secretive than males and probably why their home territories are smaller than those of males. Raising cubs is a time-consuming business—a female may devote anywhere from two to four years for each litter, and sometimes even more. If a female with young at her side does encounter a male, she will fight him fiercely, but despite the willingness of mother bears to defend their young, male bears are responsible for up to seventy percent of all young bear deaths.

Bears of all species are fascinating creatures, both to watch and to study. No wonder they attract our curiosity like few other animals in the world.

BLACK BEARS

NATURAL HISTORY

American black bears *(Ursus americanus)* are the medium-sized bears that commonly roam through most of North America's forested terrains. Black bears are plentiful from California chaparral thickets to the piñon-pine forests of New Mexico and Arizona and northeastward to the tall conifer forests of Maine. They exist in every Canadian province except Prince Edward Island. Between one hundred thousand and two hundred thousand of the animals inhabit Alaska. It is not unusual for black bears to forage in open areas. This is particularly true above the northernmost tree line, where human interference is minimal, and during spring, when bears are driven to consume fresh green grass.

Black bear numbers are soaring as the twenty-first century gets under way. Population estimates are higher now than perhaps any other time in history. Noted bear researcher D. F. Williamson recently estimated that North America's 1989 black bear population was between 625,000 and 757,500 animals, while in 1996 the estimate jumped to between 735,000 and 941,000.

The black bear population in North America in 1996 was estimated at 941,000 individuals, which was a twenty five percent increase over 1989's estimate. (photo: Courtesy: M. R. James)

Mexico, where black bears once thrived, has only a remnant population in its northernmost regions. Some Mexican bears migrated into Texas, where they established a small breeding population in Big Bend National Park.

Black bear numbers appear to have stalled in the southeastern United States, although a few populations seem to be growing somewhat.

The American black bear has for many years been hunted for sport as well as for food, fur, and other body parts such as its gallbladder, bile, paws, teeth, and claws. The latter five items continue to be sold commercially, even though laws forbid selling these items in many circumstances. Some nuisance black bears are hunted down and killed, too, but even in the face of these threats, black bear populations continue to rebound, perhaps because for every negative action toward the black bear, there is an offsetting positive action. Today strict regulations govern the methods used to take black bears. In some locales, most notably Ontario and Colorado, spring bear seasons have been closed because of concerns that too many females with cubs were being harvested.

Black bears are surprisingly adaptable to human encroachment into their territory. In Pennsylvania, some have even been found denned up beneath the homes of residents, and neither bear nor resident seems the worse for it. The demand for black bear licenses grows with each succeeding season. Luckily, black bear numbers are growing as well. The only real downsides to hunting these fascinating animals are that permits are becoming more expensive almost everywhere and in some places obtaining a permit is becoming more difficult.

Black bears are doing well in part because almost every state and province bans trafficking of bear parts. Hunting seasons, although becoming somewhat longer, remain fairly short, and sows with cubs are generally provided protection. Harvest data are compiled in great detail so that state and provincial wildlife agencies can track population trends. In recent decades, state, provincial, and territorial authorities have become more precise about controlling harvests, usually through the imposition of strict seasons, mandatory licensing of hunters, reporting methods, and regulation of hunting methods. Some states have banned highly efficient methods of hunting black bears such as hunting over bait, hunting with hounds, or both.

Black bears are far more numerous than brown bears, and that might cause them to be regarded with less respect. People seem surprised to learn that these black bears are sometimes predaceous killers of humans. Observers tend to underestimate the black bear's strength, agility, and quickness. They look at a black bear and see a clownish animal sometimes trained to wrestle with people, dance, or even ride a bicycle. People may become careless. Some have gone so far as to push or shove a wild bear out of their way. Compounding the problem is the fact that when bears are habituated to people, their level of tolerance to humans can sometimes be quite high. Yet bears will take just so much, and nothing more. Exceed their breaking point and you will know it.

Black bears, like all bears, are extremely intelligent. They are curious and will fool with something new until they master it. Researchers have spent years and fortunes attempting to perfect bear-proof trash receptacles as well as methods of aversive conditioning designed to teach bears not to mess with humans. Whether the latest generation of "bear-proof" trash containers will live up to its description is anybody's guess, but bears to date have been winning this battle of wits.

Black bears are also opportunists. They will never turn down a handout, whether you know you're giving them one or not. As long as the animals are not injured, it is remarkably easy to habituate most black bears to the presence of people, vehicles, and homes. Black bears will roam about under cover of darkness investigating everything there is to see near a dwelling. If it is not frightened or hurt during this initial investigative process, it may return with an increased level of confidence. In this way, black bears easily become habituated to people and conditioned to the food people leave scattered about their dwellings and campsites. When bears find food without working for it, they soon become lazy. No longer do they feel they must grub for their meals when so much tasty food can be found in bird feeders, barns, fruit cellars, and dogfood bowls. It does not take long for such a bear to attempt to break into a house, if for no other reason than to reach the sources of all the succulent aromas it can smell. If someone gets in its way, trouble is the likely result.

Behaviors

Black bears threaten mainly through bluffing and blustering, though a bear may sometimes rush in to bite or strike out with a forepaw at the object of its aggravation. When a sow feels that her cubs are in danger, she will send them up a tree. Even when cubs are left alone, they scamper up trees at the merest hint of danger. They then may climb out onto the flimsiest limbs, where they'll be safe, even from adult black bears.

Yes, adult American black bears can climb trees. This strategy comes in handy when they are being harried by brown bears, wolves, and sometimes even humans.

Hikers, campers, anglers, and hunters who choose to wear dark-colored clothing in black bear country should be aware that they may resemble black bears as they move slowly through the forest or along streams. If a curious black bear is not able to get a whiff of human odor to set the record straight, it may proceed to get very close indeed. Once they identify the distinct human scent, most bears will flee, but if a bear mistakes a person for another bear, an attack can result.

Attacks on humans usually occur for one of two reasons. First, a female may be protecting cubs, which can lead to an extremely dangerous situation, particularly if she is habituated to people and is food conditioned. Second, a black bear with no human experience may regard people as possible prey. This circumstance is thought to be the reason for attacks by so-called predaceous black bears.

Range and Habitat

Black bears inhabit much of Canada and large portions of the United States. As we went to press, twenty-eight states and ten Canadian provinces and territories permitted black bear hunting. Almost all states and provinces report either stable or growing black bear populations, which seems to prove that with proper wildlife management, black bear numbers increase, even when the bears are hunted.

Roughly forty thousand black bears are legally harvested in the United States each year, and yet bear populations in most areas continue to grow. The estimated annual revenue generated from the sale of bear tags and hunting licenses equals or exceeds $30 million. Our Canadian neighbors each year harvest about six per-

Roughly 40,000 black bears are legally harvested in the U.S. each year. Dwight Schuh is the lucky bowhunter in this photo. (Courtesy: Ron Dube)

cent of their black bear population, while U.S. harvest data indicate that each year about three percent of the total black bear population is legally taken. Many more black bears could be taken from both countries with no adverse effects on the population.

Now, at the start of a new millennium, black bears are migrating into places where no bears have been seen for a century or more. Several states where bears were either no longer found or were extremely rare seem to be gaining bears, including Ohio, Missouri, and Kentucky. Forty-one states as well as ten provinces and territories report resident black bears. States with no black bears, or too few to estimate, include Delaware, Hawaii, Illinois, Iowa, Kansas, Nebraska, North Dakota, Rhode Island, and South Dakota. The only Canadian province or territory to report no black bears is Prince Edward Island.

Black bears are threatened in Florida by fragmentation of their habitat. Plenty of unoccupied bear habitat exists in this state, and although bear numbers have been increasing and bears are slowly repopulating these areas, human development shows no sign of abating.

Threatened subspecies include the Louisiana black bear. Since Minnesota black bears were stocked in Louisiana at one time, some biologists question whether a pure strain of Louisiana black bear even exists. Most biologists believe that some pure-strain black bears remain, particularly in the extreme northeast portion of the state near the Texas National Wildlife Refuge, as well as in the extreme southern parishes of Iberia and St. Mary's.

Only the occasional black bear is reported across the Mississippi River from Louisiana in east Texas. This area is so close to Louisiana and the range of the threatened Louisiana black bear that each appearance piques the interest of biologists, who believe remnant bears of this subspecies may have taken refuge in east Texas woodlands.

Almost eighty percent of the estimated U.S. black bear population can be found in just eight states. Alaska alone accounts for thirty to forty-five percent of U.S. black bears. Other states reporting twenty thousand or more include Washington, Oregon, Idaho, California, Maine, Montana, and Minnesota. No estimate was forthcoming from Wyoming, but this state's black bear population probably also is very substantial. Black bears are doing well in this country, and that is good news. That news is tempered, however, when one learns that the black bear's range once stretched unbroken across most of the continent, while today's range is seriously fragmented in some areas, particularly in the southern and eastern United States.

About seventy percent of Canada's entire black bear population is in British Columbia, Ontario, and Quebec, making those three provinces the best bets for black bear hunters. Although black bears inhabit the vast Northwest Territories and the Yukon Territory, only about six percent of the estimated Canadian population may be found in those provinces, primarily because the habitat is generally poorer here. Newfoundland is yet another province with few bears in relation to its size. In fact, Newfoundland's neighbors, Nova Scotia and New Brunswick, contain more bears per square mile of habitat than any of the three provinces of Northwest Territories, Yukon Territory, or Newfoundland. Yet, this is still far fewer per square mile than there are in British Columbia, Ontario, and Quebec where habitat is lush and food sources are many. Nunavut was not yet established at the time of the last population survey (it's been a territory only since April 1999) and so is not included in charts and totals. Factors limiting black bear numbers within any area include climate and availability of high-quality forage and denning areas.

Black bears have traditionally been forest dwellers. They may have been driven into the forests during prehistoric times by short-faced bears (a now-extinct species) and grizzlies, which stood and fought rather than retreating. Such aggressive attitudes are foreign to the normally mild-mannered black bear. Although the short-faced bear has been missing from the scene for many years and the grizzly has been extirpated from most of the lower forty-eight states, it has taken almost a century for the black bear to start venturing freely into open areas where once it almost certainly never would have been found.

SIZE

Black bears, on average the smallest of the North American bears, can range in size from almost diminutive to huge. An average adult stands only twenty-nine to thirty-six inches at the shoulder and measures fifty to seventy-five inches from nose to tail. All bears have short, stubby tails, and the black bear's is no exception, measuring only about two inches in length. A boar is typically larger than a sow. In the spring, adult males weigh between 130 and 450 pounds. In the fall, after having foraged all through the summer and early autumn, adult bears usualy will gain an additional twenty to thirty percent of their springtime weight to tide them through the lean days of winter.

A few black bears attain a huge body size. The largest black bear on record as being taken by a hunter weighed 660 pounds. Older, unsubstantiated records indicate that even larger black bear specimens existed at one time. The great naturalist Ernest Thompson Seton wrote of a nine hundred-pound stock-killing black bear that was removed in the 1920s from Arizona by officials of the U.S. Biological Survey. A Manitoba black bear captured at a dump site in 1987 tipped the scales at 803 pounds before it was released back into the wild. Wisconsin's old records support the claim that an 802-pound bear was

Some black bears are huge, like this Wyoming giant that squared seven feet, six inches and was harvested by outfitter Ron Dube. (Courtesy: Ron Dube)

taken there in 1885. The *borealis* effect, a scientific rule of thumb, should provide hunters in search of huge-bodied black or brown bears with a general guide, although it's not strictly true in every circumstance. In effect, it says, "Go north for larger-bodied bears and south for smaller-bodied individuals."

LONGEVITY

Some black bears live well into their thirties, which is extremely long-lived for most North American wild game.

COAT COLORS

Some black bears really are black. But this fascinating creature's coat can range from the color for which it was named, with no white markings whatsoever, to long, silky coats of platinum blonde, cinnamon, auburn, chocolate brown, blue, and even white. Black bears are the norm in the eastern U.S. and Canadian provinces, while the very rare white or creamy coloration phase *(Ursus americanus kermodei)* can be found at the opposite end of the continent on Kermode Island, Gribble Island, and other nearby north-central British Columbian coastal locales. Even on these islands, black remains the predominant color for ninety percent of the local population. Only about ten percent of the population at any given time can actually be called a true Kermode bear, even though the Kermode gene for whiteness is as liable to be carried by an all-black bear as by one that is white. Kermode bears are white, but are not albinos. Albinos are characterized by a total absence of pigment, while pigment is present in both the skin and the eyes of the Kermode. Kermode bears have been revered from time immemorial. Native Americans honored them with the name "spirit bears." These bears continue today to fascinate anyone lucky enough to glimpse one, and have been rewarded for the beauty of their coats with total protection.

The black bear's rare blue (glacier) phase *(Ursus americanus emmansii)* is found primarily in Alaska's Yakutat area, but some are also known to exist in northern British Columbia and portions of southeastern Alaska. Glacier bear coloration occurs randomly in bears of these areas, and it is impossible to protect these animals by simply not shooting them since even bears that are completely black can carry the glacier bear coloration gene. If two such black bears mate, one or more of their offspring will be blue, so there is no benefit to protecting this population. A glacier bear sow will often be seen with a litter of all-black cubs, again illustrating the futility of trying to protect these bears to preserve this rare and beautiful color phase.

The undercoat of the glacier bears is a rich blue-black, while the outermost guard hairs are long and either white or light yellow, with silver tips. This color variation probably evolved during the last ice age, when the population was isolated along an unfrozen section of the coastline, and was the result of *genetic drift*— random fluctuation in the gene pool of a small population. The glacier's blue-gray color is an ideal natural camouflage against a backdrop of ice.

Glacier bear numbers seem to be declining as black bears without the rare blue gene migrate into the Yakutat area of southeastern Alaska. Conditions are excellent for black bears there, so there is nothing to prevent natural dispersal of animals without glacier bear genes into this area. Sadly, this dispersal may dilute the rare blue gene pool to such a great extent that the color phase will become even rarer in future years and eventually may die out completely.

Some states and provinces are noted for their variety of black bear colors, so if a beautiful and unusually colored bear hide is important to you, check with state and provincial wildlife agencies before planning your hunt. Each year thirty percent of those who hunt black bears in Montana, for instance, bag animals with coats that aren't black. Alaska is also home to many color phases. While black is the most common color, brown or cinnamon bears are often encountered in south central Alaska as well as the state's southeastern mainland.

In addition to the differences in overall color among black bears, a bear sometimes sports a patch of white hair—a "blaze"— on the front of its chest.

If an unusual-colored bear hide is important, check with state or provincial game officials before planning your hunt. Some areas are famous for producing color phases other than black. (Courtesy: Larry Heathington)

IDENTIFICATION

Size is a poor predictor of whether a bear is a black or a grizzly. Some black bears dwarf the average grizzly or small brown bear. Since these animals sometimes share the same geographical area, range is also not a surefire way to identify them either. Relying on either method—or even both—may get you a summons and a high-dollar fine from the local game department.

Black bears are most easily distinguished from brown and girzzly bears by their straighter facial profile as well as their shorter claw length. Black bear claws are sharply curved, and seldom do they measure over one and one-half inches in length. No hunter is going to shoot or not shoot a bear based on its claw length, though— if you are close enough to see a bear's claws, you are probably already in trouble.

Keep in mind that a grizzly has a distinctive hump on its back as well as a concave "dish" in its face. If you're unable to tell what species of bear you're about to shoot, then simply don't shoot.

Don't feel bad if you are unable to make a positive identification. So many hunters have been befuddled trying to distinguish between these two species that some states now require all black bear hunters to pass a bear identification course. The course has been so successful in Montana that the number of hunters buying black bear licenses has increased significantly.

If your bear is on the ground and you're suddenly unsure what you've taken, remember that grizzly and brown bears can be positively identified by measuring the upper rear molar. This tooth is never more than one and one quarter inches long in the black bear, and it is never less than that in a brown or grizzly bear.

FORAGE

Black bears, no matter where they may be found, enjoy similar food choices. When they first emerge from hibernation, they seem to crave freshly sprouted green vegetation, particularly grasses and sedges. Biologists believe bears gravitate to these types of foods for their laxative effect after the animals' long winter sleep. During their hibernation, bear respiration, heart rate, and metabolism slow dramatically. Body temperature drops only slightly, from five to nine degrees Fahrenheit. Were a bear's body temperature to fall below 68-degrees F, it would suffer cardiac arrest. Bears no longer east to support systems that have entered dormancy, so waste production ceases.

The first bowel movement the bears pass in

Black bears emerging from hibernation crave freshly-sprouted green vegetation such as grasses and sedges. (Courtesy: Jim Zumbo)

the spring is likely to consist of hard, dry scats. If sometimes may consist of a single scat between seven and one-half and eleven inches in length. Such initial scats produced after denning are commonly called fecal plugs, although no evidence supports the popular notion that the feces actually plug the bear's intestinal tract. In all bears, this fecal plug most often consists of hair, grass, leaves, and twigs, or the very materials the bear may have accidentally swallowed during the building of its den or the grooming of itself or cubs.

Although green vegetation is the most popular meal in the spring, bears are creatures of opportunity and will readily take anything they encounter. Winter-killed animals are readily eaten, and bears are cannibalistic on occasion, but carrion is apparently eaten only if little else is available. As summer progresses, a black bear's food preference shifts to salmon if it is available. In areas without salmon, bears rely primarily on vegetation throughout the year. Berries, especially blueberries, are an important late summer and fall food item.

BREEDING BEHAVIORS

Black bears mate almost anytime from May to July, depending on where they are found. Other than getting together to mate, black bears live a solitary existence except for sows with their cubs.

After a gestation period of about seven months, mothers give birth to cubs in their dens while in a state of dormancy. Cubs weigh less than a pound at birth and are blind and nearly hairless. By the time they follow their mother outside the den for the first time, they weigh about five pounds and their coats consist of a woolly covering of fine, downy hair. Litters commonly consist of two cubs, but anywhere from one to four may be born.

Cubs usually remain with their mothers through the first winter following their birth. In environments where living and finding food is difficult, they may stay for an extra year.

Bears are sexually mature at three to six years of age. Having adequate quantities of high-quality food seems to speed up the rate at which they attain sexual maturity.

Black bear sows do not breed as long as their cubs remain with them. In excellent bear range this means that sows breed once every two years. In more marginal habitats, they breed only once every three years. If a sow loses her cubs early during their first summer, she will breed again that year.

WINTER DENNING

No bear actually hibernates in the true sense of the word. Rather, they enter a state called dormancy. Not all bears enter dormancy; in some places males remain active most of the year, and bears living in the tropics don't go dormant.

The reason scientists call this period of rest and seclusion "dormancy" and not "hibernation" is because a bear's metabolic rate does not drop as much that of an animal that enters true hibernation. And unlike true hibernators, bears can awaken at any time during their dormancy.

In southern portions of their range, bears will sometimes emerge from their dens while it is still winter. In northern portions, they may remain dormant for as long as seven to eight months. Females with young usually emerge later than solitary bears.

Bears use dens from areas at sea level to above the timberline. They will hole up in rock cavities or even in hollow trees. A black bear's den is often a hastily self-made affair that is sometimes little more than a hollowed-out nest in a dirt bank or under a rock. Some bears have been discovered sleeping away the winter in little more than a slight depression dug into the ground.

HOME RANGE

In its strictest sense, a territory is simply a defended home range. Most American black bears are not territorial, although territorial behavior has been observed in adult female black bears in Minnesota, Alberta, and Montana. In a 1987 Minnesota research study, for example, Dr. Lynn Rogers, a well-known black bear biologist and behaviorist, found that adult female black bears actively defended their home ranges and would chase intruders out of their territories. Regardless, most bears do not defend their home ranges because to do so would require a tremendous expenditure of energy. Such vigilance as well as the high level of aggressiveness that would need to be sustained soon would become counterproductive to the bear's health and ability to survive.

Most black bears travel through a large home range. A typical female might range over anywhere from one to fifteen square miles. A male's territory is usually larger than a female's and will often overlap the territories of several other bears. The typical male black bear's home range may cover anywhere from eight to forty square miles, depending on the density of bear numbers, as well as the quality of available forage and habitat. Since most black bears do not defend their home ranges, ranges will often overlap. It is not uncommon to find a number of different black bears using all or select portions of another individual's home range. As bears move around in their daily activities, most often they will try to avoid each other. Should a confrontation occur, relative rank in the local hierarchical structure most often will determine the outcome.

Always remember that each bear is, above all else, an individual that is behaviorally flexible. A bear will always adopt the strategy that works best for its own benefit.

BLACK BEAR BEHAVIOR AND SIGN

Hunters who target bears soon learn that spring black bears are most active at dawn, while during the summer they'll move during daylight hours. In autumn, you may see them almost any time. Autumn bears are compelled to eat whatever they can to pack on pounds to help tide them over during their long winter dormancies.

SIGN

Black bears enjoy bathing in creeks or streams, love to wallow in the mud, and like to scratch their backs.

Like whitetails, black bears communicate with each other using scent, sound, and sight. American black bears are the most vocal of the bears.

Black bears also wander their territories, marking them as they go by rubbing their bodies on objects such as saplings or trees. Sometimes they stand on their hind feet and rub their backs up and down large trees. Other times they straddle saplings and rub them with their belly fur. Tufts of black or brown hair clinging to tree bark or underbrush will help you identify places where bears have been laying down scent.

Bears, like whitetails, seem to particularly enjoy scratching and marking trees that have a natural aroma, like cedar, juniper, and fir. Perhaps the added olfactory signal augments the visual elements of a scratching post in some way not yet fully understood by biologists. Good rubbing trees are used over and over again for decades, and even centuries. Such rubbing trees, which are usually conifers, show smooth, worn bark. Look on the ground near such rubbing trees. Twin depressions in the soil indicate where a

A black bear's marking tree is not only a visual signpost, but an olfactory one as well. (Courtesy: Jim Zumbo)

17

bear stood on its rear feet while rubbing its back and belly against the tree trunk.

A bear sometimes stands erect, reaches as high as possible up the trunk of a tree, and then rakes the tree trunk with its claws. Such marking works not only as a visual signpost that other bears can readily see, but also as a olfactory marker since the bear leaves behind a generous helping of scent while leaning hard against the tree.

Bears mark trees in three ways: by clawing, biting, or scratching their bodies against them. Trees with soft bark, such as aspen and birch, reveal every detail of bear claw marks.

While bears may leave five claw marks per paw print, often the little toe does not make a mark. Bear claws are blunt and two- to three-tenths of an inch wide near their tips.

When a bear climbs a tree, it kicks its hind claws into the bark, leaving five neatly placed puncture marks that form an arc. Its front paws make longer slices in the bark at an angle approximating forty degrees from the vertical. Longer, near-vertical cuts indicate where a bear has slid down a tree's trunk. Such slide marks are usually left by the front claws.

Bears can be extremely aggressive. They will readily fight other bears and animals to protect a kill or, in the case of male bears, to defend his right to breed a nearby estrous female. Female bears will fight to defend their cubs as well as frighten off other intruding females. Fighting, however, is used only as a last resort. Bears have an arsenal of frightening visual signals at their disposal to be used as soon as a given situation starts to deteriorate. An antagonistic bear usually will run the gamut of these signals— such as standing on its hind legs, raising its hackles to 'increase' its size, baring its teeth, roaring, popping its jaws, clacking its teeth, forcefully stamping its feet upon the ground, or bluff-charging. A bluff charge is when a bear runs at another bear (or human) but stops short of making actual contact. Such signals used alone or in combination serve to

A black bear's hind paw generally averages about seven inches in length and four inches in width. (Courtesy: Jim Zumbo)

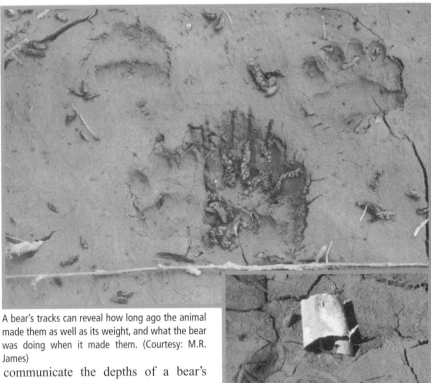

A bear's tracks can reveal how long ago the animal made them as well as its weight, and what the bear was doing when it made them. (Courtesy: M.R. James)

communicate the depths of a bear's resolve and are extremely useful in the species survival strategies.

Violence between bears can quickly lead to severe injury and sometimes even death. Nature, therefore, has equipped the animals with alternate courses of action , should they choose to use them. Bears usually stop well short of inflicting physical harm upon one another, thanks to the inherent checks and balances that probably have been genetically programmed into the species during millions of years of evolution.

An average adult male black bear's forepaw measures about four inches long and four inches wide. A trophy-sized boar's front paw usually leaves a track four and one-half to five-plus inches wide, but sometimes even more. Its hind paw will average seven inches long and four inches wide. A black bear has been endowed with short claws for an important reason: Short claws are better suited for climbing than longer claws, and climbing trees is one of the black bear's first lines of defense and escape. For this reason, when a black bear leaves tracks, usually, but not always, the marks of its claws are not visible, although claw marks may appear in wet sand or mud when a bear weighs enough to sink in and leave a complete imprint.

Scat can help a hunter determine what a bear was feeding on. (Courtesy: M. R. James)

Examining a bear's tracks through soft earth, sand, or snow can help a good tracker determine how long ago the tracks were made as well as the animal's weight, general size, and what it was doing at the time.

Scat, otherwise known as fecal matter or droppings, provides another clue to the black bear's presence within an area. Old-timers used to say that any bear scat larger than two inches in diameter belonged to a grizzly. Dr. Stephen Herrero, author of *Bear Attacks*, considers this method of identification unreliable. The criterion overlooks completely the possibility that smaller scat might be deposited by smaller grizzlies, or that scat of two inches or more in diameter might well have been deposited by a large black bear which have been known to weigh as much as a grizzly.

Scat can reveal what bears have been feeding on. Hunters may discover scat with remains of ripe berries, acorns, or beechnuts, or darker, smellier scat left by a bear feeding on meat or carrion. Once hunters identify a food source visible in fresh scat, they can start searching for favored bear feeding grounds.

Fresh scat should also serve as a warning sign to anyone who hunts bear. If you find fresh scat, the bear isn't far ahead—and it's never a good idea to walk up suddenly on any bear.

BAITING BLACK BEARS

Baiting is a great way to hunt black bears. At present, black bear baiting is legal in Maine, New Hampshire, Michigan, Wisconsin, Minnesota, Wyoming, Idaho, Utah, Alberta, Saskatchewan, Manitoba, Ontario, Quebec, Newfoundland, New Brunswick, and Nova Scotia. Baiting is also allowed to a limited degree in Alaska.

During the 1990s, animal rights extremists teamed up with preservationists and other like-minded factions whose followers believed that baiting black bears was unethical and should be made illegal. They set about to convince the general public that shooting a baited bear was like shooting a fish in a barrel, and to some extent they succeeded. Voters in Colorado, Oregon, and Washington, swayed by such rhetoric and video clips, went to the polls, where they passed measures banning the hunting of black bears with bait or dogs.

When hunters in other states became aware of what was going on, they counterattacked. Sportsmen-led coalitions in Michigan and Idaho have preemptively struck by crafting—and successfully lobbying for—legislation that prohibits putting to a popular vote any issue pertaining to wildlife or its management. Had hunters not become proactive, the domino effect would probably have toppled baiting and dogging throughout North America.

Baiting's proponents argue that whether bait is in the equation or not, black bears are appetites on four legs. That is true, particularly during the first few weeks after they leave their winter dens and during hyperphagia, the four- to six-week period of ravenous eating immediately preceding winter denning. Opportunists they are, wandering woodlands and meadows searching for food. The hunter who sets up close to a grove of beech trees or oaks just dropping their mast, or

Hunting over bait is the method of choice for many first-time bear hunters. (Courtesy: M. R. James)

near a ripening berry patch, apple orchard, or other natural food source, is attempting to capitalize on the black bear's voracious appetite as well as its tendency to never pass up a free feed. Such predictability helps explain why many bear hunters sweeten the pot with bait and experience no moral dilemma while doing so.

Hunting over bait is the method of choice for a great many first-time hunters. "Bowhunting over bait means an archer is set up perfectly," said M.R. James, noted bowhunter, as well as found and editor emeritus of Bowhunter Magazine. M.R. has been bowhunting black bears for well over thirty years in many different states and provinces. When he speaks, other bear hunters tend to listen, "A baited bear usually provides the bowhunter with a close, perfect shot at a relaxed, motionless animal. Why would anyone be against that? Close shots at standing game means fewer wounded animals. The bowhunter has time to decide whether the bear is big enough or see if it's a sow with cubs tagging behind her."

M.R. noted that more Pope and Young bears are taken with bait than with any other method. "You get a lot of time to size a bear up," M.R. said.

GO WITH AN OUTFITTER, OR DO IT YOURSELF?

Hunters who bait bears soon realize that time is a critical factor. "Unless you have a lot of time, as well as a place to hunt bears near your home, tending a bait doesn't make a lot of sense," said M.R. "It's more efficient to have a bait set up and bears working it before you begin to hunt. That's the advantage of hunting with a guide or outfitter. He can have the bait set out and ready before you ever leave home."

Not to mention having nothing to do but hunt once you arrive! It's easier to keep your mind on hunting when you don't have to worry about keeping the black bear goodies flowing. Hunters who book with a lodge or guide can often sleep in a real bed, enjoy home-cooked meals, and take hot showers.

Guides have different ideas about what kind of bait attracts bears. M.R. has hunted with guides who put out twenty pounds of stale pastries or cookies. "One of the neatest guys I've ever met is from the 'less is more' school," M.R. said. "Plenty of guides will put out a hundred pounds of meat to lure black bears. My friend does the opposite. His favorite bait is a combination of corn syrup, french-fry grease, popcorn, and fish entrails and other parts. Above the bait he'll hang an attractant concocted of beaver castor and other vile-smelling oils and juices." M.R. said that it's fairly easy to get used french-fry grease from local fast-food restaurants. "You're saving them the money they'd have to pay to have someone haul it away," he noted.

The do-it-yourself bear baiter must adhere to a steady regimen of backbreaking labor from midsummer through hunting season. Hauling stinky bait into the backcountry can quickly become boring, although some hunters gladly put up with any inconvenience for the chance to hunt bears.

"My favorite bear bait is popcorn," M.R. said. "Popcorn is light, so it's easy to pack to your treestand. Sprinkle cinnamon or salt on it, and bears love it. I'll also soak a nearby log with french-fry grease or corn syrup and then climb into my stand."

A hunter who uses popcorn as bait can carry everything in one or two plastic buckets. Merely scattering bait around, however, is no guarantee of success. "There is a tremendous difference between hunting an area under a lot of (hunting) pressure and hunting one where there is very little," M.R. commented. "If bears are pressured, they may run in, grab the bait, and race off. They are wired to move quickly since they are shot at all the time.

"Take the time to walk over another ridge or go a little farther to get away from the hunting pressure," he advised. "That way you'll use a minimal amount of bait with good results."

Baits that have been tended over many seasons become part of the local bears' cultural knowledge. With their excellent memories, bears know what baits they have been feeding on as well as when to return to forage there again. Such bait sites will

Log cribs like these arranged around the bait cause bears to stand either broadside to the hunter or quartering away. (Courtesy: M. R. James)

attract bears all season long, particularly in areas of good bear density with little hunting pressure. Some animals travel great distances to see what new and delectable treats are awaiting them. Neophyte bear hunters enjoy seeing lots of animals, and most are not too disappointed if many of the animals are rather small.

POSITIONING BAITS

Most baits should be positioned so that hunters in treestands between eleven and fifteen feet above the ground will be between ten and fifteen yards from the bait station. Even at such close ranges, killing a bear cleanly requires perfect arrow placement. A bear's vital zone measures roughly eight inches square and lies just behind the its front shoulder. A poorly hit bear may run off, as a deer does, but the similarity to deer ends there. While a deer may bed down and bleed out, a bear won't. A bear's will to live is incredibly strong, and a poorly hit bruin will usually run until it dies, which means your search area will encompass square miles rather than square yards.

"Contrary to what some people believe, baiting bears is not like shooting fish in a barrel," emphasized Wyoming outfitter Ron Dube. Ron outfitted black bear hunters for years in the Bighorn Mountains. "Baiting is challenging, because bears have an extremely refined sense of smell. I was watching a bear once with its head buried in a stinky carcass. As I was waiting, the bear lifted its nose, sniffed, and shot out of there like a scalded cat. Now, there is no way that bear should have smelled me, not over the stench of that rotting carcass. But it did."

HUMAN SCENT

"Sensitivity to human odor may have something to do with how wild the bears are," Dube mused. "These bears were truly wild. They were not used to having people near them. They were so spooky, it took us a long time to get them accustomed to the bait. They were too worried to come in and feed freely. It was especially hard to get them to come while there was still enough daylight to shoot."

"In heavily hunted areas, bears can be tremendously spooky," M.R. said. "That being said, I don't go out of my way to worry about wind. I've yet to be convinced that unpressured bears worry much about human scent."

M.R.'s approach to human scent is the opposite of Ron Dube's. "Even if you wear rubber boots and odor-adsorbent clothing, it's impossible to keep yourself odor-free enough to fool a bear," said Ron. "A bear has one of the two best noses among North American game animals. I just don't think you can trick them most of the time, so why try? Bears are cocky. They're at the the top of the food chain. A bear will be either overconfident and not worried about human scent or hungry and not worried about it. Either factor will lead to its downfall."

M.R. said he's watched spooky bears attempt to come in on a bait. "They'll catch my scent, whirl, and run," he said. "Most of them will do this a few times, then try to come in from another direction. A bear, no matter how scared, will usually work in closer. It'll be cautious and wary, but it'll continue to try because it's hungry, or it craves what's in the bait barrel. If I want the bear, I know that it will present me with a good shot. If it doesn't, that's okay, too. I don't ever want to take a risky shot on any bear."

Whether hunting with a rifle, shotgun, black-powder gun, or bow, a bear's fur is so thick and woolly and its fat deposits so substantial, that entrance and exit wounds often clog soon after the bear is hit. Matted hair and huge globs of fat block these wounds and halt blood flow. With no blood trail, the hunter's work is tough. Bear tracks may be more difficult to detect than those of deer, especially in dense undergrowth, leaf litter, grassland, or rocks. Tracking a wounded bear is a real art.

Baits should be placed so they provide hunters with a good broadside shot at any visiting bear. (Courtesy: M. R. James)

Bear Baiting with an Outfitter—What to Expect

An outfitter who advertises baited hunts for black bears can be either sublime or awful, and all points in between. It's your responsibility to determine, before you send a deposit check, what type of outfitter you're booking with.

As soon as you arrive in camp, your outfitter will probably check over your license to see if it is in order. He or she may look over your gear or ask about your gun. If something seems fishy or your gear seems inadequate, a good outfitter wants to know about it, and the sooner the better.

After the gear check, you may draw for treestand locations or baits until all the hunters know where they'll be hunting the first day. Many outfitters have more than enough baits for all of their hunters. If they do, they may simply assign each hunter to a bait or baits. Repeat hunters may receive preferential treatment from an outfitter when it comes to bait or stand selection. That is the outfitter's prerogative.

Baits should be positioned to provide you with a good broadside shot at any feeding bear. The bear's vital zone should not be obscured, and a clear shooting lane should exist from the treestand to the bait station.

Whether the outfitter positioned the treestand prior to your arrival or you positioned it yourself, check it again each time you prepare to climb into it. Too many hunters die, are paralyzed, or become seriously injured because they fail to take the time to look out for their own safety. Here is a simple checklist:

- Don't assume a treestand won't fall just because it was positioned by an outfitter.

- Always wear a safety harness—even when climbing into and out of the stand.

- Make sure you can hang your bow or gun on a hook or a limb. It's better to hang up your weapon so that if you nod off, you won't drop it and possibly shoot yourself or break your bow. Consider packing a removable screw-in or strap-on hanger to take with you no matter where you plan to hunt.

- Never trust tree steps. Test each one as you go before commiting your entire weight to it.

- Keep a variety of bungee cords in your pack to help stabilize poorly positioned, wobbly, or rickety stands. If you still do not feel safe, consider constructing a ground blind of limbs and brush instead of hunting from a tree, but check with your guide or outfitter before doing so, since black bears can be dangerous.

Attractants

If you cannot set out baits before a hunt, you may find yourself with a limited amount of time in which to attract a bear. Improve your odds by trying various scents. In areas where it is legal, undiluted oil of anise attracts bears like catnip lures cats. Soak a rag in the oil, then hang it from a wire high enough off the ground that small animals cannot reach it.

Or try a bacon burn. Fire up a can of Sterno or another portable heat source, and fry several strips of bacon. Pour the hot grease and bacon over a nearby log or over your bait-cover logs (bait-cover logs are placed on top of a hole that contains bait), being careful not to start a fire if conditions are dry.

A honey burn can also work like a charm. Pour an inch of honey into a clean tin can. Light a burner on a propane stove, and set the tin can over the flame. Heat gently for ten minutes, then increase the heat until the honey is billowing clouds of white smoke. Cook until the honey burns and black smoke is streaming from it. Turn off the heat, leave the burnt and smoking honey on the stove, climb into your stand, and wait.

If you are preparing to open a bait or attract your first hit to a bait, burn the honey on top of the bait barrel. A honey burn works best the first time it is used at a bait. Delaying a honey burn's use until later in a hunt is wise, especially if you have time to spend on stand. If you choose to make a honey burn, do so, and then get back into your treestand right away. Bears will usually appear shortly after a burn is finished.

Bob McGuire, a bowhunter from Tennessee who wrote a first-class book on hunting black bears, *Black Bears: A Technical and Hunting Guidebook,* classified three types of bear bait:

1. Portable hangers include grease and scent bags hung high out of reach. These are the baits you'll be most likely to use during a short bear hunt.

2. Ground baits are great in states or provinces that do not allow barrel baits. A "carcass set," for example, is made by wiring an animal carcass to nearby trees to prevent bears from dragging it off. Another variation is the "pit bait": Dig a hole, dump bait inside, and then drag logs over the pit to keep any animal but a bear from getting to the bait.

Claw marks are common on trees near bait sites. (Courtesy: M. R. James)

3. Permanent containers such as a metal drum into which small drainage holes have been punched in the bottom an inch or so up the barrel's sides. Where legal, permanent containers are well worth your while. Place fresh bait inside the barrel. Cover the bait with logs that fit inside the drum. Weigh down the bait with logs and then with a few heavy rocks. The additional weight will help deter skunks, raccoons, and other animals from freely feeding. It will also help to alert the hunter when the bear gets rambunctious and knocks the barrel to the ground. (Sitting for long hours over a bait barrel can inspire even the most stalwart hunter to take a short nap.)

Barrels (or other metal containers) can also be positioned on their sides with the bait placed as far inside as possible. When the bear sticks its head in to get the bait, it will forget everything else, and you can prepare to shoot without the its ever knowing you are near.

Always secure bait barrels to trees or boulders. Otherwise, bears may roll them off or carry them away.

Bear baiters sometimes dump a gallon or more of used french-fry grease all around a bait barrel, six inches or so from its metal bottom. Any visiting bear steps into this oil and dirt goo and then tracks the scent of oil all over the countryside, which attracts even more bears.

FAVORITE BAITS

Bears love sweets: sticky buns, cookies, pastries, and doughnuts are all favorite treats. They also enjoy red meat, beaver carcasses, fresh beef bones, honey-soaked bread, fruit, and grease.

The drainage holes in the bottom of the bait barrel will keep odor-nullifying water off the bait—but if baits become too dry, they sometimes quit smelling. If you can't detect the proper bait "aroma," try freshening the scent by sprinkling the bait with a little water from your canteen.

TRACKING SAND

The trophy hunter may want to place a layer of sand on approach paths some distance from the bait. If a bear ventures close to the bait for a sniff or a bite, the sand will reveal its tracks. Any bear with a pawprint larger than six inches is a bear worth hunting.

BEARS' AGGRESSIVE TENDENCIES

Bears are big, and they can be mean. When riled, most are afraid of nothing and no one. Hunters feeling safe sitting in their stands should always remain aware that bears can turn on them—and quickly.

"I've seen too many black bears that were sitting on their butts yawning one minute, then bluff-charging you the next, not to respect these fellows," said M.R. James.

Meat, pastries, and used cooking oils are favorite bear baits. (Courtesy: M. R. James)

"Bears can be unpredictable, even those you've been watching dig around in the bait barrel for a couple of days," he continued. "I've shot two bears that became very aggressive and threatening. They raised their hackles and tried to climb into my treestand with me as I was watching a bait station. One tried to get in with me three times, popping its teeth and just generally threatening me. I finally killed that bear.

"I killed another equally aggressive black bear that was hanging out between me and my boat. I didn't really relish

A smelly, stinky bear bait may be just the thing to attract ravenous fall bruins. (Courtesy: M. R. James)

the idea of climbing out of my tree in the dark and then trying to walk to the boat with this aggressive black bear hanging around.

"After I shot them, I discovered that one of the bears had a severely infected paw," M.R. said. "It hadn't been wounded by a hunter. It was merely an injury that became infected. The other bear I killed was a big male that displayed an extraordinary amount of aggression."

Aggressive black bears will sometimes try to climb into a bait hunter's treestand.

TREESTAND TIPS FOR HUNTING OVER BAIT

M.R. James prefers to use a portable, lightweight treestand with a comfortable seat. "Bait hunters spend a lot of time in their stands just sitting and waiting," he said. "Hunting over bait takes patience. You won't stay still unless you're comfortable."

Bruce Pelletier, bear hunter extraordinaire and owner-operator of Rockford, Maine's Gentle Ben's Resort, agreed. "Our bait hunters are between sixty and seventy percent successful," Bruce said. "It would be closer to one hundred percent *if* I could get them to sit still."

"I don't like a wobbly stand," M.R. continued. "I'll fasten or secure my stand with belts or straps so that there is no way it will move, shift, or squeak. Strange noises will make the bear constantly glance in your direction. That won't help your cause. The bear will remain on edge, and you may never get a good, relaxed shot."

"I prefer a strap-on ladder for my treestands," M.R. said. "Bears are so curious. If you use strap-on steps, they will chew on them and just really mess them up."

Baiting bears successfully is both an art and a science. Hunters like Ron Dube, M.R. James, and Bruce Pelletier have spent their lifetimes refining all the nuances of the sport. As much as they already know about baiting black bears, all three agree that they have barely scraped the surface of what remains to be learned.

Hound Hunting

Strenuous for the Dogs and for You

A bear hunt with hounds may be the most exciting and physically demanding hunt you can make. Whether you follow the hounds through deep western canyons or struggle through vast forests with branches whipping at your face, you must be aware that bears have an almost limitless supply of places to run to or hide in, and they know these places as intimately as the backs of their paws. When you're contemplating this type of hunt, remember this: Wherever the bear leads the dogs, you must follow.

Hound hunting, like hunting over bait and spring bear hunting, is under constant attack from animal rights activists. Yet hound hunting provides hunters with an excellent method of determining a bear's size and sex. If for any reason the bear is not what the hunter is after, it can be left alone to run another day.

Most houndsmen now outfit their dogs with radiotelemetry collars so the dogs can be found if they are injured, if they run off, or if they simply travel out of hearing range. Such devices also help guides guard against possible dog theft. Hunters searching for a true traditional hunt with hounds, where there is little reliance on modern gadgets or technology, may not approve of such devices, but from the houndsman's point of view, it's hard to risk losing a good bear dog, possibly worth several thousand dollars, that might have been recovered had it been wearing a radio collar.

"In my opinion, only a hunter who is in top physical shape should undertake a hound hunt for bears," stated Jim Zumbo, noted hunting authority and award-winning outdoor writer. Jim, who is also a degreed wildlife biologist, has hunted bears all over the West. He knows what he's talking about.

Check with your outfitter ahead of time to learn whether the hunt will be conducted on foot, on horseback, or mainly from vehicles. Chasing after bears on foot or horseback usually means a wild and woolly hunt. One of my hunting buddies, the late Charlie Wolter, always told me that the most strenuous and dangerous hunt he'd ever been on was a rugged horseback bear chase through western canyon country. Several times bears managed to evade the hounds entirely after the outfitter and his hunters had ridden many miles at

Hunting black bears with hounds can be the most physical hunting of all.

breakneck speed, often through twisting piñon-pines or thick underbrush that whipped at the men and tore their clothing. Charlie was able to kill his bear only after enduring a hard eight-hour race through winding canyons, up rimrock ledges, and across the high desert. "I can tell you this," he related. "I really earned that bear." Unfortunately, this type of hunt is becoming harder to find in many western states, as in one state after another hound hunting and bear-baiting are banned. The method is still legal in some states, though—New Mexico and Idaho, for example—so be sure to check on its legality where you plan to hunt before contacting an outfitter.

"I've hunted bears behind hounds a couple of times," Jim Zumbo said. "Some of the places we got ourselves into were simply too rugged, too steep, or timbered too thickly to allow anyone to ride through on a horse. I was never so winded in my entire life.

"There's no hanging back, either," Jim continued. "If the bear bays on the ground—and bears, unlike cougars, don't always tree—the dog handler and his hunters have to keep up—otherwise the bear may kill all of the guide's expensive hounds."

Hunting behind hounds might be too much for someone who is just getting into hunting. Most neophytes have enough trouble merely sitting still long enough in a treestand to let an animal get within range. Add the din of baying dogs and the possibility of shooting at an enraged bear that may be actively battling the hounds, and it may be more excitement than a rookie can handle.

But if you're up for a strenuous, devil-may-care gallop through unknown territory, or if you believe you're in good enough shape to light out on foot through forests and creeks, and over hills and mountains, then you'll want to find an outfitter proficient in one or both of these methods.

LESS-STRENUOUS BEAR HUNTING

More-sedentary bear hunters may opt for outfitters or guides who use radio receivers to track the dogs as they give chase. Rather than expect hunters to endure a possibly futile and energy-sapping races with time, these outfitters follow their hounds' sounding or track the signals being transmitted by the hounds' radio collars until they determine that their dogs are barking "treed." At this point, outfitters use a four-wheel-drive vehicle to drive the hunters as close as possible to where the the bear is cornered; then they'll all travel the rest of the way on foot.

Not even this type of hunt will always be easy. Sometimes the walk may be over reasonably level terrain. More often, though, it won't be a "walk" at all, but will entail some serious climbing and rough travel through steep, unruly terrain. Seriously out-of-shape hunters should check beforehand about the hunt's difficulty level. If it sounds like too much to handle, hunters should probably book a hunt for black bears over bait.

In many cases, the guide's ethics will dictate that all hunters race behind the hounds for one of the most exciting escapades in all of hunting.

A DAY IN THE LIFE OF A HOUND HUNTER

If dogging a bear sounds like a perfectly great way to hunt, here's how your day will unfold. The hunt will start early in the morning after the hounds have been rigged for the chase with radio collars, if legal, and the leashes they'll wear until they are turned loose on a scent. You follow the hounds, and when they sound off, you know they've scented either a bear or a place where a bear recently traveled. At this time they are released and the hunt begins in earnest.

Some guides and outfitters maintain baits where dogs will be taken to see if they pick up a fresh scent. A good start dog, which is a dog that knows from experience to track the bear in the direction in which the bear left the bait site, and not in the direction from which the bear approached the site, is then brought forward to sniff the area around the bait station. As the start dog picks out the bear's retreating track, the rest of the hounds are released to head out on the bear's trail, barking "here and there" before exploding into sound when they actually locate the bear.

You and your guide follow as quickly as possible on foot, muleback, or horseback. Your mission: to keep the hounds within hearing distance. If you can no longer hear them, your guide may contact the hunting camp or fellow guides to see if they can hear the dogs. Black bears can run with suprising speed. They have incredible stamina, and they are remarkably agile. These animals are fully capable of crossing a stream atop a small, fallen log that stretches from bank to bank. When they execute this maneuver, few if any dogs will follow. A bear may also run in the water to confound the hounds. The dogs may sometimes pick up the track again, but not always, particularly if the bear remains in the water for a considerable distance.

Races after bears can be as short as thirty minutes or as long as a day, so be prepared for any eventuality. If you've booked with an outfitter who is well prepared for this type of hunt—and it is legal to do so—he or she will have more than one pack of hounds—possibly three or more, depending on state law— so fresh dogs sometimes are available to relieve the trailing pack when the dogs tire. Of course, guide and hunter will tire as well. In that case, sometimes a second guide will remain on the trail. Once the bear is treed or otherwise stopped by the hounds, the hunter and the first guide will catch up. The dogs' barks change once a bear climbs a tree or is bayed, and the guide can detect this change instantly. If all goes well, the hounds will be able to hold the bear long enough for you to collect your trophy.

Not all bears are particularly worried by hounds, though. On occasion, they move quite slowly, which makes for a more leisurely experience. Don't expect such good fortune, though—expect the worst and you'll never be disappointed.

Once the animal is down and field dressed, the outfitter or guide will begin the process of deciding how to get the animal back to camp. In some cases, you and the guide may pack the bear back to the truck—that is, after you find the truck. More and more, modern outfitters are depending on Global Positioning Systems (GPS) to help direct them not only back to their trucks or the hunting camp, but even to downed game in the field or to where their horses have been tied. GPS units are a godsend to outfitters. These handy technological marvels have saved outfitters, guides, and hunters many a leg-weary hour already, and they've been available for only a few years.

SNAGS TO WATCH OUT FOR

Beginning houndsmen must carefully consider all the ramifications of a hound hunt on foot or horseback. Besides the legality of using dogs to run bears within a particular state, there is also the question of whether it is legal to use dogs on the tracts of property a bear may cross during the chase. Bears do not respect property lines. They can easily get onto private property where hunting permission may not have been granted, and some property owners may be less than thrilled to see you come barreling through behind a pack of howling hounds.

Bear dogs don't always stay on the bear's trail, either. They might decide to chase property owners or their pets instead, or gulp down dog food property owners have left out for their own animals. Hounds may even inspire perfectly well-behaved pets to leave their happy homes and join in on the fun. If you are considering getting into hound hunting, don't be surprised to run afoul of property owners unless you have taken the time to clear potential chases ahead of time and have given them a heads up to get their animals inside and away from the temptation of the racing, baying pack soon to come.

Finally, check with your outfitter about possible rate changes should you fail to bag a bear. A few outfitters don't charge if a client returns home without a bear, but you should never demand a refund. Such decisions are best left to the outfitter's discretion— only he or she knows what costs were incurred during your hunt.

IS HOUND HUNTING FOR YOU?

Some hunters simply love to hear the baying of a pack hot on the trail of a wily old bruin. Those who enjoy hunting with dogs or training hounds will naturally gravitate to hound hunting.

Some states permit group hound hunts for black bears. Pennsylvania, for example, allows as many as twenty-five hunters to follow a pack. Hunters who enjoy the camaraderie of running bears in a group will wonder why it took them so long to try hound hunting for bears.

Others, though—those for whom hunting is most satisfyingly spent in silence and contemplation or who pride themselves in making difficult shots—will be disappointed with a hound hunt. Hound hunting is exciting, but it's not quiet or contemplative. And while hunting bears this way may call for some skill with a gun, it doesn't take much, since the bears are usually treed quite close to where hunters stop.

Hunting black bears with hounds can be an exciting and challenging hunt. It can be as short as thirty minutes or as long as a day. (Courtesy: Ted Rose)

Nevertheless, some hunters enjoy hound hunting more than anything else in the world. For them, nothing compares with a brisk chase listening to the hounds race through the backcountry, hot on the heels of a big black bear.

SPOT-AND-STALK HUNTING

OPEN GROUND STALKING IN CANADA AND ALASKA

Outfitters who guide hunters along Canada's and Alaska's northernmost fringes of trees often spot black bears feeding on gut piles remaining from early season caribou or moose hunts. Some outfitters advise caribou hunters to purchase black bear tags to take advantage of a great opportunity for a two-species bag. Spot-and-stalk works especially well if your quarry is a trophy black bear boar. A nearby tree line indicates forest beyond, and the few scattered thickets of trees that extend onto the tundra afford big bears enough cover to make them feel secure. Barren ground tundra is often gently rolling,which also increases the bears' comfort level. Hunters should like this country as well—the dips and swales provide needed cover when they're putting the final stalk on trophy bruins.

Once breeding season ends in June, most adult boars leave the forest to wander about on the open tundra. They pass the time foraging on bush blueberries, bog cranberries, and subalpine blackberries. Bears will eat as much ripe fruit as possible at one location before moving on to another. This lethargic lifestyle suits larger bears just fine, and the animals steadily gain weight until autumn. Their summer weight gain, while substantial, still isn't sufficient for an animal that will soon shut out the world for several months. As days shorten, the looming winter inspires black bears to go into a literal feeding frenzy. The animals chow down on anything and everything that might increase vital stores of body fat for the long winter's sleep ahead. Gut piles left behind by late summer caribou hunters provide a source of premium protein with minimum effort. The value-to-cost ratio tilts significantly in value's favor, making gut-pile feeding a good deal for the bears. Some trophy black bear hunters book or plan a hunt for both black bear and caribou in areas where seasons overlap just so they have a chance to capitalize on this late-season bruin tendency.

One might argue that open-ground stalking near gut piles is nothing more than glorified baiting. That isn't true. Where gut piles are both many and scattered, there's no telling where black bears may appear. Some may feed only at night. Others may start to feed on one gut pile and then leave for another. Bear movements in areas of wide open spaces are more random and unpredictable than near actively tended baits. This simply adds to the challenge of the hunt.

When hunting barren ground black bears, start glassing within optical range of the northernmost tree line. (Courtesy: Jim Zumbo)

Knowing that a plethora of gut piles exists as winter approaches means many black bears throw caution to the wind. It's not unusual to spot several of these big, shaggy creatures roaming the open tundra in broad daylight, searching for meat. Wise hunters will outfit themselves with good optics, situate themselves at an excellent vantage point downwind of several gut piles, and start glassing within optical range of the tree line. After bears gorge themselves, they'll usually lie up in the timber while their meal digests. The first twinge of hunger will send them looking once more to the tantalizingly fresh piles of offal.

Whether you choose to spot from one of the huge boulders that commonly litter much of this country or simply perch behind a substantial tundra knob is a matter of preference. The idea is to attain a high enough elevation downwind of the feeding grounds to spot bear movement. There is nothing more thrilling than watching several huge old bruins lumber from their temporary woodland lairs as a brisk north wind ripples their long, silky coats.

Barren ground country is just that: barren ground. This is some of the last land that opened up after the glaciers' retreat at the end of the last ice age. Boulders that were deposited as the glaciers melted dot much of the landscape. After you spot a big bruin in terrain like this, your next task is to keep the wind in your favor as you slip close enough for a shot. Putting a boulder or a small tree between you and the bear as you sneak toward it is one workable technique. So is staying hidden in the folds of the earth as you work your way ever closer. As winter nears in barren ground country, the wind picks up. When you're stalking bears, the wind may be your ally, but it can also be your enemy, because shooting accurately in windy conditions requires you to get reasonably close to your target.

Once the caribou-hunting camps shut down for the season, bears are drawn closer to them by the smell of blood from abandoned meat houses as well as the smell of cooking that permeates the now-empty kitchens. It is common for black bears to break into these camps and wreak havoc. Buying a bear license for a late-season hunt could buy you a chance at one of the bruiser bruins that are out and about at this time of the year.

Spot-and-stalk for black bears can be used successfully anywhere black bears travel through open ground. The best circumstances occur when a bear is leisurely feeding or grazing in an open area where it won't be harassed by others and possibly chased off before you can put the stalk on it. Larry Heathington, a former bear guide and outfitter from Arizona, sometimes used spot-and-stalk tactics in the fall as bears were gorging themselves on favored foods before denning up for the winter. "I'd cover a lot of territory with my hunters," Larry said. "Early each morning we'd take the pickup and drive to various backcountry spots. I'd park the truck, and then we'd walk to places where from past experience I knew we'd find big prickly pear flats. You have to come at these spots from downwind, and ideally you want to be high enough to be able to look over a lot of country. Bears are fairly easy to spot in such places. They really stand out. Morning is when bears are reluctant to leave the prickly pears they've been feeding on, and some of them just wander in for a while before they lie down for the day. Once you spot a bear you want to take, stay put and watch where it lies down. Then just come back later that afternoon to where the bear was that morning and wait for it to get up. That's when you can bust it."

One other place to find bears in the fall is foraging in oat fields. If you know

Ex-guide and bear expert Larry Heathington used spot-and-stalk tactics each fall when bears were gorging on prickly pears. (Courtesy: Larry Heathington)

bears have been in a farmer's crop fields, don't be afraid to ask permission to hunt. Most farmers and ranchers regard bears as nuisance animals. Not only will they allow you to hunt, but they may even help you by telling you where to start searching.

SPOT-AND-STALK IN THE TIMBER

In areas where black bears occur, they range between open and forested areas—they seem to have no "druthers." They go where the food is—or, if it's mating season, where the sows are. And as winter approaches, they search for den sites.

Hunters in the northwest region of the continent often ride back roads or highways where they glass every forest opening or logging trail where bears might be spotted. Black bears seem to like walking along logging roads. When they leave their dens, they often head for these roads to graze on the young sprouting grass or budding clover whose seeds are frequently sown by timber companies in the fall to prevent erosion. Many timber companies permit hunters access and hunting on their lands, but always double-check beforehand with local game and fish personnel or law enforcement agencies.

Remington's Linda Powell and noted outdoor humorist Pat McManus pose with Pat's B.C. black bear. (Courtesy: Jim Zumbo)

Black bears can sometimes be spotted standing or walking in streams or traveling along stream banks, too. The U.S. Forest Service manages vast tracts of timbered wilderness where hunting is allowed in accordance with state wildlife laws. Be armed with an up-to-date map of any area you plan to hunt so that you don't run afoul of private property owners.

When searching for black bears along logging roads and streams, remember that most states and provinces prohibit shooting from the sides of public roads. The statutes in each state are different, so be sure to find out well ahead of your trip what is legal and what is not.

The very nature of the forest makes spot-and-stalk hunting more difficult in densely timbered areas. Most hunters who kill black bears in heavily wooded tracts do so by chance. Deer, elk, and moose were the primary objectives of many successful bear hunters, who bought over-the-counter bear tags as an afterthought. Such hunters sometimes bagged bears after spotting them by chance while searching for their primary targets or after unexpectedly finding themselves within shooting range of them.

In many areas of the country, spot-and-stalk bear hunting in the timber is considered a very chancy proposition. In a few areas, though, black bear outfitters and hunters actually concentrate their spot-and-stalk activities in timbered areas. Such hunts most often find hunters and guides using spotting scopes to survey rock slides where local bears enjoy searching for grubs, lichen, or moss. Such areas also are preferred in the spring, when bears crave shoots of tender, green grass shortly after emerging from their winter dens.

Some outfitters have good luck guiding hunters to bears feeding on south-facing slopes in the spring. Bears seek out such areas because that's where the snow melts earliest and the year's first green growth pushes through.

Springtime bruins may also seek out other favorite foods—the buds, leaves, and catkins of aspen trees—so keep aspen thickets in your sights, too, particularly those that are just budding out.

You can use a similar tactic in early fall, when rolling hills are covered with ripe berries. Bears are sometimes so preoccupied with feeding on the berries that you can stalk close enough for a clean shot, but you must pay constant attention to the wind. Getting close enough to make the shot with a bow can be one of the most challenging experiences in all of hunting.

Once you spot a bear, you and your guide put the sneak on it. Such a stalk may pay off, but it may also fail because of erratic, swirling mountain winds that make it almost impossible to predict with accuracy the direction in which human scent will blow. Wearing scent-blocking garments or using scent-elimination products could help get you close enough to make the shot.

Wearing scent-blocking garments could help you get close enough to make the shot on a black bear. (Courtesy: M.R. James)

STAND HUNTING FOR BLACK BEARS

Never discount the effectiveness of hunting black bears from treestands, even if you are not allowed to use bait. Dalton Carr, a former government bear hunter and one of the country's preeminent authorities on bear hunting, is sold on stand-hunting, especially in the fall. "Bear hunters can really do well when hunting from stands during periods of drought," he said. "That's the time to set up near water holes or other water sources bears use. If the countryside is dry, bears won't be feeding on berries or acorns, because both of these mast crops need water to mature.

"Another good black bear tactic during droughty times is to set up near an elk herd," Dalton continued. "Black bears go into a feeding frenzy for about a month before they hibernate. They have to pack on weight so that they can survive the winter. If other types of forage are scarce, bears will start lurking near elk herds. They'll be forced to kill elk calves and stragglers when the opportunities present themselves, or they themselves will be in danger of not surviving the winter."

CALLING BLACK BEARS

The premier caller of black bears in North America is Larry Heathington, formerly of Casa Grande, Arizona, and now living in Texas. Larry is well-known as an outfitter who really knows his stuff, whether it's hunting bears, sheep, pronghorn, or any number of other big game species. Larry accompanied Chuck Adams when that bowhunter killed his record-book Alaska brown bear that squared or measured ten feet, eleven inches. Larry has also guided ex-publishing mogul Robert E. Petersen on most of his hunts, many of which involved Foundation of North American Wild Sheep auction tags or high-dollar governors' tags, and almost all of which resulted in Petersen killing Boone and Crockett record-book rams, pronghorn bucks, or Rocky Mountain elk. "I haven't been hunting as much during the past few years," Larry admitted. "I prefer to arrange and guide two to four high-dollar hunts each year and spend the rest of my time training and showing cutting horses."

During his years as both an outfitter and guide, Larry traveled from Arizona to Canada hunting black bears with clients. Somewhere along the way, he hooked up with Reed Carney, a hunter who had experienced good luck calling bears. "I sure didn't figure bear calling out. Reed pioneered the technique. He was using a varmint call when a couple of bears came in. Bear calling just took off from there."

In fifteen years of hunting, Larry Heathington called in over one hundred bears for lucky hunters like this man. (Courtesy: Larry Heathington)

43

To call in bears, Larry uses a call that mimics the scream of a rabbit. His favorite brand is Circe. "This call has ejectable reeds, so it's quick and easy to replace them," he said. "Calling bears means doing a lot of calling—pretty much nonstop for about forty-five minutes at one location. You then walk fifteen or twenty minutes to another place and call from there for another forty-five minutes. If you continue to call like this all day long, you'll find a bear that will come in. Look out, because when they do, their hackles will be standing on end and they will be mad. They sometimes rush in so close, bouncing their front paws off the ground, that the hunter sits there sort of stunned. I always told them, though, if the bear isn't big enough or is not the right color, shoot at their feet or between their front legs. That scares them off.

"Calling works," Larry said. "In over fifteen years of hunting, I called in more than one hundred bears, and more than fifteen or sixteen of them squared eight feet or more. That's a big black bear for Arizona." Terry Paysom, one of Larry's hunters, killed one huge black bear boar with an estimated age of twenty years. The old boar squared eight feet, eleven inches, immense by black bear standards. "The oldest bear was a twenty-four-year-old sow, well past the age when she could have cubs," he said. "She was blind in one eye. A sow too old to have cubs will really put on weight, so it's difficult to determine whether they're sows or boars. An old three-hundred-pound sow could pass for an eight-year-old boar."

Larry's calling sometimes worked almost too well. "I once guided Wyman Meinzer, the Texas wildlife photographer and writer," he said. "I told Wyman to get ready, but I'm not sure he believed me. He'd said he wanted to get some close-up shots of a big bear. I asked, 'How close?' He said, 'As close as you can get 'em.' Well, okay. I first called in a brown one, but then a blonde bear came in. It came closer and closer and closer, and finally Wyman yelled, 'That's close enough!' Well, he'd said he wanted the bear in his face. I guarantee you, he's got photos of a wild bear from about six feet away."

Larry doesn't feel too guilty about calling bears close enough to make friends and acquaintances distinctly uneasy. "I called in one bear for Bill Cross, a good hunter and one of my best friends," Larry recalled. "That bear came in very close, and did so extremely quickly. It scared Bill so badly he never guided bear hunters or went bear hunting again. He said, 'I'm done. I'm too old. I'm not as fast as the bears are, and I'm done.' He was, too."

Larry has called bears equally well during both spring and fall seasons. "Calling works pretty much by rote," he said. "I'd hunt public land anywhere there was a fairly substantial population of bears. I'd position my hunter or hunters out on the rimrock so that the bears would have to come in from below and the hunter would have a good, unhurried shot. The best laid plans, however, don't always work. Sometimes bears would sneak in from behind, too.

"One day I was guiding Terry Paysom," Larry continued. "I was calling and we both were watching down-canyon. I heard a twig snap and turned around to see a big old sow trying to clamber up the rimrock to get up to where we were. I said, 'Terry, do you want this bear?' He didn't, so we scared her off."

Larry was quick to point out that black bears don't always play by the rules. "Sometimes everything would work perfectly," he said. "You'd spot the bear several hundred yards off and have plenty of time to get into position to make the shot. Other times, though, they'd be on top of you before you even knew they were there. That's why you get up high on that rimrock so you can see into the canyon below. Bears can be sneaky. You must watch everywhere. They'll sometimes come in behind you, or to the side of you, and they'll even come in two or three at a time. That really keeps things interesting."

Larry said that during more than fifteen years of guiding, he called in about fifteen black bears each year. "Calling near a big prickly pear flat where bears can feed works well," he said. "They really love eating prickly pears."

Larry said that calling works well all day long. "There's no best time," he stated. "The first bear I ever called in responded at 2 P.M. What I'd usually do was go out early in the morning, call for four or five hours, then return to camp for lunch and a nap. After we'd slept a while we'd go back out to call and hunt some more. This was very effective, because you were hunting all day long."

Larry rarely guided bowhunters. "Heck, when I was guiding back in the 1970s and 1980s, archery wasn't that big yet," he said. "I wouldn't recommend using a call for a bowhunter. When a bear responds, he's already mad. A bowhunter who made a poor shot would just make matters worse."

Bowhunters shouldn't be upset because Larry feels this way. He's not even too keen about calling in bears for some of the firearms hunters he's guided. "That's the problem when you're guiding bear hunters," he said. "They're not always as quick with the gun as you'd like them to be. That

A tree stripped of its cambium layer proves black bear have been using the area. (Courtesy: Ron Dube)

means you have to run into the brush a lot to escape an angry bear."

When he was still guiding bear hunters, Larry advised them to use any caliber from a .270 Win on up. "I'd pack a .338 loaded with 250-grain soft-nose bullets as a backup gun," he said.

"Bears don't scare me much," Larry continued. "I've had lots of close calls. I once was looking for a wounded bear. I walked right past the place where he was hiding in the brush. He charged out of there and ran at me from behind, busting brush as he came. I spun around and shot and killed him in midair. His momentum carried him past me, and as he rolled by, I had to kick his carcass off me. That was too close. It made me a lot more cautious."

Larry could regale you with exciting bear tales for hours. "One bear tried its best to get me," he said. "It came charging uphill at me. It didn't get there, but he sure did his best. Another time I was guiding Jim Callahan, a gunmaker. Jim had never before killed a bear. We spotted one standing on a ridge about five hundred yards away. I pulled out the call, and before we knew it, here came the bear on a dead run. It came in so fast Jim couldn't get a shot off quickly enough. Before we knew it, the bear had leaped up onto the same rock ledge we were on, and was still running directly for us. When Jim finally shot, the bear was just twenty yards distant."

Larry said bears seem to respond to calls better when the sky is overcast and drizzly. "Bears like cool, cloudy weather better than hot, sunshiny days," he said.

According to Larry Heathington, black bears can see movement farther than most people think. (Courtesy: Larry Heathington)

"In the springtime, if it starts snowing again, don't give up hunting. Bears will not return to their dens if they've already blown their plugs." That simply means returning is not an option once bears have eaten enough to initiate digestion, which eventually results in defecation. A brown "plug" of fecal matter indicates that that year's hibernation is over for that particular bear.

If Larry has a regret, it's that he never tried calling bears in Minnesota or Wisconsin. "I always wanted to crawl into a treestand and call," he said. "I know it would work."

As for bears themselves, Larry has nothing but respect for them. "Bears can see movement way farther than you think they can," he said. "Move or make noise, and they damned sure will hear or see you." To counteract possible fidgeting by his hunters, Larry advised them to wear camouflage from head to toe, and then told them to sit still.

"I didn't use a spotting scope and I never relied on binoculars," he said. "I always looked with my naked eye. If bears are coming, you're probably going to see them. They really stand out—those big black or brown or blonde blobs coming through the green weeds or trees. The hardest time I ever had making out a color was once when a hunter killed a platinum blonde bear. I could barely see it because in the fall the oak brush was kind of yellow and the bear's coat blended right in."

Larry lived and breathed bear hunting for a good portion of his adult life. His advice on shooting at a bear is simple, and can be broken down like this: "Shoot through both shoulders and bust 'em down if you can," he said. "The bottom line is that you don't want the bear up and moving around. If it can't move but is still alive, you can always shoot it again. If it's moving, though, you'll have a devil of a time finishing it off."

For those who want to try calling, which is probably the most exciting bear hunting experience of all, Larry offered this tip on shooting charging bears: "Use the top edge of the upper scope cap as your sight when a bear is charging at you, and you'll get him," he advised. "This is such a good way to sight on close objects that you can even use this trick to shoot an eight-inch plate at twenty-five yards. Calling bears that may pop up extremely close to you presents real problems to hunters who have scopes on their rifles. Even if the power ring is turned all the way down, there's still enough magnification to screw you up. That's no good when a bear's about to run right down your throat."

Larry has some tips about how to maintain your calls, too. "When you call this much, number one, you've got to have some pretty good lungs on you," he said. "At first, two hunters should probably switch off, or someone is going to be pretty winded.

"Second, plan on replacing your call's reed—perhaps several times in a day. I always packed spares, and that's why Circe's call is so good. Because the reeds are ejectable, replacing them is no problem. You'll blow lots of reeds out of the calls, too, but I always kept two calls on a lanyard around my neck. When one call would stop working, I'd switch to the second. While using the second call, I'd replace the reed in the first. That way you're giving any nearby bears the constant stimulation they need to provoke them into coming to see what's going on."

According to Tom Beck, a retired bear biologist who formerly worked for the Colorado Division of Wildlife, each year he gets reports of successful bear hunters who bagged their animals after luring them into range with a deer call. "Fawn bleats seem to work best," Beck said, "but the distress call of any animal that shares a bear's range would probably be effective." Although somewhat off the topic, each year a number of Sitka blacktail hunters in northwestern Alaska generally will report various harrowing brown bear encounters after the hunters try to use deer calls to lure a buck close enough to shoot.

Larry didn't have any cut-and-dried advice concerning when an Arizona hunter would get the best bearskin on an animal. "Really, it depends on the bear," he said. "I've seen poor hides in the fall and poor ones in the spring. If you want a good hide, I'd advise you to go as late in the season as possible. By that time their winter hairs are all grown out, and hides should be prime. And if you go hunting in the spring, you probably should go as early as possible to get a hide in good condition. In my experience bearskins are really ratty for only about thirty days each spring."

Larry Heathington has done it all when it comes to hunting, guiding, and outfitting for trophy-class animals of many species. He has nothing left to prove in this arena, so he has left it for a while to devote time to another of his loves, the training and showing of cutting horses. He'll never get hunting totally out of his blood, though, and that's a good thing for us hunters. As long as Larry is willing to share, all hunters will continue to discover exciting tactics like calling for trophy black bears.

STATE BEAR HUNTING REGULATIONS

The black bear license you apply for or buy over the counter will help to determine how you will hunt these animals. Through the years, nonhunters and many folks who love animals have come up with some strange notions about how to manage wildlife, including bears. One small Missouri municipality outside the city of St. Louis recently hired a man to trap some of their deer and relocate them because of citizen complaints over damage to their landscaping. Nothing strange about that, you may think. Until you discover that the trapper was ordered to trap animals in family groups. For every doe the trapper caught, he also had to catch the doe's young and a buck—the "father" of the "family."

Anyone who's wildlife-literate realizes that a buck stays with a doe only until she's bred. He then moves on to another doe with which he may breed. Demanding the trapper to catch and release white-tailed deer in family groups qualifies not only as foolish, but also as counterproductive.

Bears also are the recipients of such anthropomorphic notions, partly because they seem like humans in some ways. Bear cubs are cute and cuddly, and people

Always refer to the wildlife code where you are hunting before baiting black bears. (Courtesy: M. R. James)

seem to feel some kind of connection with them. In a few states, this "connection" has resulted in the appearance of wildlife management issues on voters' ballots. In some places, people can no longer hunt with bait or dogs, both of which have probably been used since people lived in caves. But nothing seems to slow down those who believe they have the bears' best interests at heart. Do these folks ever stop to consider how wolves and bears themselves kill their prey?

It is lucky for hunters that bears can be taken by methods other than bait and dogs. Bears are becoming so numerous that some hunters purchase a bear license wherever they hunt, just to be prepared should a bear wander within range.

Despite increasing restrictions on hunting methods and seasons as well as steadily escalating license costs, more black bears are harvested each year. What's even more surprising, black bear populations continue to expand into new areas, and black bear numbers seem to be increasing in most parts of their range.

AL	No listed season*
AK	Must be at least 16 years of age to register a bait station; other restrictions regarding location apply; some locations may be closed to black bear hunting; only black bears (NOT brown bears or grizzlies) may be baited; no shooting while bears are swimming; no cubs, or females accompanied by cubs may be taken; no dogs** may be used, except under limited circumstances, while hunting black bears.
AR	No bait; no dogs; no disturbing denned bears
AZ	No females with cubs; no bait; dogs okay for bears and mountain lions
CA	No cubs or females accompanied by cubs; no dogs during the archery season for deer or bears
CO	No dogs; no bait; no spring bear hunting; no killing bears with one-year-old cubs
CT	No listed season
DE	No listed season
FL	No listed season
GA	Dogs, some restrictions; no females or cubs under 75 pounds; no bait
HI	No listed season
IA	No listed season
ID	Dogs okay; bear baiting permit (with applicable rules) required
IL	No listed season

IN	No listed season
KS	No listed season
KY	No listed season
LA	No listed season
MA	No bait, no dogs
MD	No listed season
ME	Restrictions on bait; no dogs in open firearms season for deer; no more than four dogs
MI	No training or hunting with dogs in certain locations on certain dates; no chasing with dogs during the archery-only season on certain dates in specific locations; some bait site and date restrictions; no taking of cubs or females accompanied by cubs; no disturbing bears in dens
MN	No white bears may be taken; no dogs; bait restrictions apply and bait sites must be registered
MO	No listed season
MS	No listed season
MT	No bait, no dogs
NC	No salt, no bait, no cubs, no females with cubs
ND	No listed season
NE	No listed season
NH	Bait requires a permit; there are date restrictions on bait; dogs require a permit
NJ	No listed season
NM	No bait; dogs okay
NV	No listed season
NY	No bait; no dogs
OH	No listed season
OK	No listed season
OR	No females with cubs less than a year; no one-year-old cubs; no bait; no dogs
PA	No bait; dogs cannot chase big game; no scents; no lures; no parties greater than twenty five persons; no killing bears in den
RI	No listed season
SC	No use of bait to concentrate bear population or lure bears to give the hunter an unnatural advantage; party dog hunts for bears must register; no Sunday big game hunting in specified wildlife management areas

SD	No listed season
TN	No cubs or females with cubs seventy five pounds or less at side; there is a bear dog training season no permit required
TX	No listed season; no hunting of bear
UT	Dogs okay; no hunting; bait restrictions apply
VA	No bear hunting with dogs in specified locations and during specified times; there is a bear hound training season; no females with cubs; no bait
VT	Permit required to hunt with dogs; there is a dog training season for bear hunting; no bait or use of baited areas
WA	No bait; no dogs
WV	No cubs less than one hundred pounds, or any bear accompanied by such a cub; no Sunday hunting; no pursuing a bear after the chase has begun with dogs not used at the beginning of the hunt
WI	Bait restrictions apply; dog training restrictions in relation to bait apply
WY	Bait restrictions apply; no cubs or females with cubs at their side; no dogs

* "No listed season" means that the state does not have dates for a bear hunting season. Bears may not be game animals in some states or their numbers may not be sufficient to warrant hunting.

** "No dogs" means no dogs for bear hunting only; there may be other rules for hunting deer or mountain lions with dogs or for bird dogs and retrievers.

Hunters remain responsible for verifying any of this information before they go bear hunting in a particular state. Regulations change, and where bears are concerned, they change rather frequently. Do NOT assume that this information is current or correct.

THE STATE OF BROWN BEARS AND GRIZZLIES WORLDWIDE

GRIZZLIES VS. BROWNS

The Pope and Young Club and the Boone and Crockett Club have established a physical boundary within Alaska to differentiate between grizzlies and brown bears. Bears taken north and east of this imaginary line are called grizzlies, while those taken south and west of this line are browns. Many hunters simplify this description by saying that any Alaska brown bear taken within seventy-five miles of salt water is a brown bear, and all others are grizzlies. All coastal British Columbia brown bears are considered grizzlies.

OVERALL STATUS

Brown bears *(Ursus arctos)* are doing reasonably well wherever the animals can be found, despite the continuing doom-and-gloom predictions of major international conservation organizations, including the World Conservation Union (IUCN). Most bear enthusiasts, naturally, would prefer to see brown bears do better, but given the rapid increase in the world's human population and the corresponding development or despoilment of some choice parcels of brown bear habitat, the situation could be even bleaker. Brown bear numbers are stable or increasing slightly almost everywhere the big bears can be found. This includes Russia, Canada, Alaska, the lower forty-eight United States, and even several European nations. In other European countries, brown bear numbers have either stalled or are plummeting. Such populations may already be in serious trouble due to genetic inbreeding.

BROWN BEAR STATUS
ALASKA BROWN BEARS

The brown bears that inhabit Alaska's coastal areas and Russia's Kamchatka Peninsula can attain a huge body size. One monster bruin, killed in 1954 by Darrell Thompson as he hunted close to Port Heiden, Alaska, was estimated by state game officials to weigh twenty-two hundred pounds. A single shot from Thompson's .375 H&H Mag penetrated the animal's chest and put it down for good. Authorities who aged the bear told Thompson his big boar was thirty-five years old, truly ancient for a bear. The creature's immense hide squared nearly fourteen feet, and from ear tip to ear tip spanned twenty-five inches. The bear's front paw width measured an astounding thirteen inches. Even more remarkable, when scored using the Boone and Crockett system, Thompson's bear's skull scored 34 9/16, which, if even remotely accurate, would blow the reigning Boone and Crockett Alaska brown bear champ right out of the water. The current world record recognized by Boone and Crockett scores an impressive 30 12/16 inches. This behemoth was killed in 1952 by Roy Lindsley on Kodiak Island just off Alaska's western coastline, where brown bears, on average, seem to grow larger than anywhere else. Photos still exist of Thompson's monster brown bear, but for some reason the skull measurements were never entered into a record book.

Despite their huge size and incredible muscle mass, the diets of both brown bears and grizzly bears consist mostly of plant matter. The animals forage on berries, sedges, hedysarum, and many other types of vegetation. The big bruisers also hunt marmots and ground squirrels; they sometimes dig for hours to excavate a few promising ground squirrel burrows. Such a bear leaves a swath of destruction in its wake. A bulldozer might do less damage. Brown bears may topple or roll huge boulders to access burrows and lay waste to a tremendous area of land during a few hours of digging. The bears also scavenge, prey on moose calves and caribou fawns, and sometimes kill adults as well. Salmon is another favorite food, and scientists theorize that plentiful salmon runs may be directly responsible for the huge size of the coastal brown bears. Once salmon enter the streams, brown bears and grizzlies alike gather to gorge on the rich, pink flesh. Scant caloric expenditure while fishing together with ample high-protein fare means the bears gain weight rapidly. When salmon are plentiful, brown bears rapidly gain weight just when they need it. By the time they begin to think about denning, most are butter-fat.

A mature Alaskan brown boar in his prime weighs somewhere between nine hundred and eleven hundred pounds. Although rare, an extremely large bear may break the fourteen-hundred-pound barrier. Most sows weigh one-half to three-quarters as much as an average-size boar.

Brown bears range through many habitat types, but most often are found in open subalpine meadows or coastal tundra. They also frequent steep mountain terrain, shrub-covered slopes, riparian zones, bogs, and heathland flats.

Recognized brown bear subspecies besides the Alaska, Siberian, Kodiak, and grizzly include Gobi and Manchurian brown bears. Safari Club International recognizes Alaska brown, grizzly, barren ground grizzly, Eurasian brown, Siberian brown, Kamchatka brown, Amur brown, and Mideastern brown bears. Most of these names reflect the region of the world in which each bear is found.

The brown bears of Russia's Kamchatka Peninsula, such as this one taken by Warren Parker, can attain a huge body size. (Courtesy: Warren Parker)

EUROPEAN BROWN BEARS

Several hundred years ago, brown bears inhabited most of Europe, although not large offshore islands such as Ireland, Iceland, or Corsica. As human population and interference increased, brown bear numbers decreased as a result of deforestation and fragmentation of habitat—the same factors driving some bear populations down today. Unregulated hunting, including poaching as well as killing bears in defense of lives or property, also took a gradual toll. Today about 50,000 brown bears still reside in Europe and Russia. Of that number, 36,000 are found in Russia. Unfortunately, in some countries bears are sliding toward extinction.

The bear is the ultimate trophy desired by almost every top Finnish, Russian, and Romanian hunter. Bears are so rare in France and Italy, though, that no one gives the animal much of a chance of surviving in those countries.

The most notable European and Russian populations include:

Good numbers of brown bears—about 37,500—exist from the eastern slope of Russia's Ural Mountains eastward to the western coast of Finland.

In Finland, bears are distributed throughout the country except for the Ahvenamaa Islands (Åland). Overharvest and habitat degradation had seriously reduced Finland's once-thriving bear population to a shadow of its former self by the beginning of the twentieth century, but bears have responded well to more stringent hunting seasons.

Estonia is home to between 440 and 600 brown bears, while Latvia has very few. The 8,100 brown bears that inhabit Slovakia, Poland, the Ukraine, and Romania collectively are called the *Carpathian Mountain* population.

The 2,800 brown bears inhabiting the forests delineated to the east by the Alps, to the north by northeastern Italy, and to the south by Greece are known as the *Alps-Dinaric-Pindos* population. This population inhabits forested areas of of Austria, Italy, Slovenia, Croatia, Bosnia & Herzegovina, FYR Macedonia, the Yugoslav Federation, Albania, and Greece.

The *Scandinavia* population includes the approximately 1,000 brown bears that inhabit Sweden and Norway. Only 130 individuals survived there in 1930, and some estimates place the present population at as much as 1,300. This population is the most productive in the world, with an annual reproduction rate of between ten and fifteen percent. Researchers remain unsure why Europe's and Russia's brown bears are so much more productive than those in North America.

The 520 brown bears that inhabit southwestern Bulgaria and northeastern Greece are known as the *Rila-Rhodope Mountain* population. Of that number, fewer than twenty-five are found in Greece.

The relatively small *Stara Planina Mountain* population—two hundred brown bears—inhabits a seventy-five-mile-wide corridor in west-central Bulgaria. During the early twentieth century, serious efforts were made here to exterminate brown bears, one reason why so few animals remain. Poaching, which increased after the fall of eastern bloc Communism in 1989, is another reason bear numbers continue to stagnate here.

Finally, five extremely small and isolated brown bear populations are found in southern and western Europe, and three of these are highly threatened with extinction. A similar population in Norway's Vassfaret area may have become extinct during the late 1980s.

In Spain, two brown bear populations totaling between fifty and sixty five individuals are known collectively as the *Western Cantabrian Mountain* population. The bears are distributed over an area of twenty-six hundred square kilometers. The population is in a steady decline due to human actions, primarily snaring to kill wild boar and poisoning to kill wolves.

Italy's *Appenine Mountain* population, officially comprises between forty and fifty brown bears today. The group of bears inhabits Italy's Abruzzo National Park as well as the lands surrounding the park. As recently as 1985 this population was thought to contain between seventy and eighty bears which indicates the severity of their declines since then.

Other small, isolated brown bear enclaves include Spain's *Eastern Cantabrian Mountain* population (twenty bears), France's *Western Pyrenees* population (six bears), and Italy's *Southern Alps* population (four bears), all of which would

Warren Parker traveled to Romania to bag this trophy Eurasian brown bear. (Courtesy: Warren Parker)

probably have been doomed without restocking efforts. In 1999, two bears from Slovenia were introduced into the Southern Alps population, followed by the release of seven additional bears during the next two years.

Brown bears are popular trophies among hunters from every part of the world. Bear researchers and biologists who have studied the threats facing European brown bear populations recently came to the conclusion that when bear hunting is legalized and becomes a source of revenue, local people seem to tolerate nuisance bears and accept their presence better. This change in attitude reduces bear poaching, one of the main reasons some bear populations are in decline.

The outlook for hunting brown bears in Europe is slowly improving. The last year for which data exist—1999—more than seven hundred brown bears were killed legally in Europe. Romania is the only European country to report that hunting is reducing the size of its bear population, but a decrease in brown bear numbers was the goal of their bear management plan.

GRIZZLY BEARS

Grizzly bear numbers probably reached a peak in North America just prior to European settlement. At that time historians estimate that more than one hundred thousand of these bears inhabited the western portion of the continent. Grizzlies ranged as far east as the central Great Plains and as far south as central Mexico, but for some reason they never traveled any farther. Two factors may have combined to limit the continued expansion of their territory. First, newly arrived immigrants were building settlements and pushing farther into once-pristine wilderness areas. Second, it is possible but not likely that black bears may have competed with grizzlies in areas where the former species was already well established.

Most North American grizzly bear populations are thought to be either holding their own or increasing slightly.

GRIZZLIES IN THE LOWER FORTY-EIGHT STATES

From a biologist's point of view, the grizzly bear is simply a small brown bear, so examining its status in this section is appropriate. Grizzly bear numbers in the lower forty-eight states, like those of the larger brown bear, are either stable or increasing in most areas of their range. Grizzlies have rebounded from an estimated low in the 1970s of about three hundred individuals to today's best guess that at least 1,100 now roam portions of Wyoming, Montana, and Idaho. This number includes a closed remnant population of about twenty-five bears that inhabit Washington's Cascade range. A good portion of those 1,100 grizzlies can be found in Montana's Glacier National Park and its surroundings, an area known as the Northern Continental Divide Ecosystem (NCDE). Farther south, reports during recent years indicate that sightings of grizzly sows with cubs within the Greater Yellowstone Ecosystem (GYE) have increased significantly. Each year one or two adventurous young grizzlies travel beyond designated recovery areas into places where the species has been absent for many decades. Not that these youngsters remain there—more often than not, they eagerly return from whence they came. But not all of them have returned, and that's a definite step forward for anyone who longs to experience a wilderness that was almost lost.

Don't look for any of the lower forty-eight states to establish a grizzly bear hunting season anytime soon. Wyoming would like to have the management and regulation of grizzlies in the state returned to its Game and Fish Department, but preservationist factions are equally determined to prevent such a thing. Anyone with a slight knowledge of brown bear population dynamics understands that the taking by hunters of one or two problem bears each season would barely register on the mortality scale, particularly if the bears were boars or older sows. Not only would Wyoming be able to sell tags for such hunts for large sums of money, which could be earmarked for grizzly habitat or studies, but the state could also assign a biologist or game warden to accompany each permitted hunter to help determine which bear to shoot, greatly reducing the chances of killing the wrong animal. Removing problem bears from the population would serve to mollify neighboring ranchers, too.

As grizzly bear recovery efforts first got under way in the mid- to late-1960s the general consensus among the managers of various government agencies, research scientists, and state and federal biologists trying to convince disparate factions of ranchers, hunters, and preservationists to work toward this common goal seemed to point strongly toward an eventual return of the bear's management to the states once certain pre-ordained population goals were attained. Ask state biologists, though, and you'll hear doubt expressed about whether such a thing will ever happen, given the federal biologists' propensity to meddle in all grizzly-bear decisions. At one point, five hundred was bandied about as the grizzly bear population the feds were striving to achieve. The population today is twice five hundred and then some, and control remains with the U.S. Fish and Wildlife Service (USF&WS) due to the grizzly bear's special status in the lower forty-eight. It apparently does not matter to those in power that neither the North American nor the world brown bear population is threatened. Instead, USF&WS not only continues to dictate policy, but they now have also expanded grizzly bear reintroduction efforts into the Bitterroot Ecosystem (Salmon-Selway Ecosystem or SSE).

GRIZZLIES IN CANADA

The grizzly bear population for all provinces combined probably hovers near the thirty thousand mark.

ALBERTA: By the 1880s, grizzlies were all but gone from their southern ranges in Alberta, where once they were numerous, although never as numerous as in neighboring British Columbia. Historic highs between nine thousand and sixteen thousand dwarf the figure of one thousand animals estimated to be roaming Alberta today.

By the early twentieth century, grizzlies could be found only in Alberta's western forest fringe. Conflicts with humans resulting in a bears' deaths, habitat fragmentation, logging, petrochemical exploration and development, and continuing human encroachment into once vast grizzly habitats all share responsibility for the great bear's decline.

Alberta residents can still hunt grizzlies. This year seventeen bears outside the parks are expected to be harvested according to Dave Ealey, a spokesman for Alberta's Ministry of Sustainable Resource Development.

The grizzlies of the Canadian plains were once found as far east as the Red River of Manitoba, but were extirpated at the time of human settlement. The only Canadian population of grizzlies to still survive east of the Rockies is found in Swan Hills, Alberta. The high elevation and dense forest of this prairie refuge is now home to about four hundred of these rare Great Plains grizzlies.

Alberta protectionists have taken a cue from compatriots in British Columbia to mount a drive to declare grizzlies endangered even though populations have been building during the past fifteen years and continue to build today. Barring any type of catastrophe, grizzly numbers will continue to increase as long as officials manage license allocations while also protecting critical grizzly bear habitats that remain.

BRITISH COLUMBIA: The relatively unpopulated areas of British Columbia are extremely important to one of the largest remaining concentrations of grizzly bears on the North American continent. Between ten thousand and thirteen thousand grizzlies—roughly half of the Canadian population—inhabit British Columbia. Prospects for their survival darken, though, when one learns that many of the undeveloped wilderness regions along the western coast are being opened for backcountry recreation and timbering. Logging means roads, and roads provide hunter access and other disturbances that lead to population declines. Only through careful management will grizzly habitat remain productive and grizzly numbers not be seriously affected by the encroachment of humankind and industry.

To help ensure the survival of the grizzly bear, the government of British Columbia has implemented the Grizzly Bear Conservation Strategy to protect this species and its habitats.

A recent campaign mounted by antihunters and preservationists led to the brief suspension of all grizzly hunting within British Columbia. That edict was abandoned after a new government was elected, although some areas remain temporarily closed to grizzly hunters.

The fate of grizzly bear hunting in British Columbia will ultimately depend upon the recommendations of a panel of experts appointed by the Ministry of the Environment.

The magical allure to be found in hunting one of the world's largest predators can be too strong to deny.
(Courtesy: Jim Zumbo)

THE NORTHWEST TERRITORIES (NWT): The NWT is home to an estimated 3,500 to 4,000 grizzly bears, with the highest concentrations found in the Mackenzie Mountains.

THE YUKON TERRITORY: The best estimates of Yukon wildlife officials place grizzly bear numbers in this territory at somewhere between six thousand and seven thousand individuals.

AVAILABILITY AND COST OF LICENSES AND HUNTS

Despite the fact that in much of their range both brown bears and grizzlies are fairly abundant, prices have soared during the recent years for all brown bear licenses, as well as for the fees outfitters now demand—and get—from those who desire to hunt them. Regardless of the high cost, outfitters who offer brown bear hunts are overwhelmed with bookings, and hunters may be assigned a hunt dates five or six years in the future. A hunter could travel to Africa and back, hunt for two or three weeks while dining upon fine china in a beautiful lodge or spiffy bush camp, take ten or more different African game species while accompanied by an excellent professional hunter and still shell out less than half the dough needed to go on an Alaskan brown bear or grizzly hunt.

That's scary.

Hunters don't seem to care what it costs to kill such a magnificent animal, though. The magical allure of hunting one of the world's largest predators is simply too strong to deny. Many hunters save for their entire lifetimes just for the chance to take one of these giant brutes on its own home turf.

Hunting Grizzly Bears

1805 May 5

Capt. Clark and (George) Drewyer killed the largest brown bear this evening which we have yet seen. It was a most tremendious looking anamal, and extreemly hard to kill notwithstanding he had five balls through his lungs and five others in various parts he swam more than half the distance across the river to a sandbar, & it was at least twenty minutes before he died; he did not attempt to attack, but fled and made the most tremendous roaring from the moment he was shot. We had no means of weighing this monster; Capt. Clark thought he would weigh 500 lbs. For my own part I think the estimate too small by 100 lbs. he measured 8. Feet 7 1/2 Inches from the nose to the extremety of the hind feet, 5 F. 10 1/2 Ins. arround the breast, 1 F. 11. I. arround the middle of the arm, & 3.F. 11.I. arround the neck; his tallons which were five in number on each foot were 4 3/8 Inches in length. He was in good order, we therefore divided him among the party and made them boil the oil and put it in a cask for future uce; the oil is as hard as hogs lard when cool, much more so than that of the black bear. The Grizzly Bear is one of the largest and strongest animals in the world, with many external and internal features.

Captain Meriwether Lewis wrote these words almost two centuries ago, during his and Captain William Clark's famed Voyage of Discovery. Grizzly bears of Lewis and Clark's time typically had had confrontations before only with various native peoples. The primitive weapons wielded by Indians never were much of a match for a grizzly, one of the continent's toughest customers. But Lewis and Clark soon discovered that the bears were terribly hard to kill even when wounded by weapons from their arsenal of "modern" weapons. Inexperienced hunters of grizzlies quake in their boots over tales such as the one above, but a well-placed shot at an unaroused grizzly will usually kill the animal as rapidly as a shot at any other large game animal. It's just that a "well-placed shot" can be difficult to make when a hunter is standing within twenty-five yards of one of these big bruisers. And that should the grizzly be aroused, then it becomes a whole different story.

The Inuit call grizzlies Aklaq. Lewis and Clark dubbed them grisly, griz, and grizzly for the grizzled or silvered appearance of their coats, and the name stuck.

Settlers often called the bear "Old Ephraim." In recent times these bears have been called "silvertips," again because of the long white- or gray-tipped hairs that give them such a distinctive appearance. Scientists, well aware of the bear's fierce reputation, dubbed the animal *Ursus arctos horribilis*, Latin for "horrible bear." The name accurately describes a grizzly hell bent on mayhem, which on rare occasions some may intend. Yet today's scientists understand that most often these animals choose to retreat rather than take their chances with humankind.

NATURAL HISTORY OF THE BARREN GROUND OR TUNDRA GRIZZLY

Although barren ground grizzlies are smaller in body size than other grizzlies, they are highly aggressive and incredibly fierce—a dangerous combination. During 2000, Alaskan officials credited these animals, also called tundra grizzlies, with ten human fatalities in an area where few humans live. The lesson is simple: Never take the barren ground grizzly too lightly.

Barren ground grizzlies were persecuted—and their numbers reduced—during the peak years of the fur trade, but during the past two decades their numbers have rebounded with vigor.

A big barren ground boar will tip the scales at more than five hundred pounds, while a large sow will weigh about half that. When pelts (pelage) are prime, the guard hairs are long and silky and the underfur is thick. The barren ground's coat can vary in hue from black to pale blond. An intermingling of white or gray hairs serves to give many of these bears the classic grizzled appearance. This grizzling is most obvious on darker-coated bears.

Fewer barren ground grizzlies are found per thousand square miles than grizzlies of other areas simply because tundra habitat is poorer. Coastal areas provide bears with a regular supply of salmon. Logs fallen or dropped amid dark timber yield a feast of termites and grubs. Out on the barren ground or tundra, food is more difficult to find, and so are good denning sites in which to while away the brutal winter.

The country these bears inhabit looks bleak and stark, yet these big omnivores subsist on a surprisingly varied diet of berries, insects, ground squirrels, marmots, lemmings, caribou, muskox, moose, and carrion. During the Arctic spring green-up and well into the early summer, barren ground grizzlies have even more to choose from, including flowers, grasses, sedges, herbs, tubers, corms, and roots.

Rob Gau, a biologist with the Northwest Territories, documented the feeding habits of barren ground grizzlies. He verified that caribou, by far, is the bears' most common food item. The most *important* items, though, are berries: crowberries, blueberries, cranberries, and bearberries. So vital is a generous late summer berry supply to the eventual reproductive success of tundra grizzlies, says Rob, that an absence or general scarcity of berries may be the primary limiting factor preventing barren ground grizzlies from expanding their range and numbers throughout the central Arctic region.

BARREN GROUND GRIZZLY RANGE

The barren ground begins just north of the last tree line and extends up to the edge of the polar ice cap. The land is exactly as described—barren ground—and it represents the very outermost margins of suitable brown bear habitat. From a distance, these barrens appear flat and almost featureless. Some creeks rush and tumble as they journey to the sea, while others slowly meander. Willows crowd the stream banks in many place, and their branches often mesh in a thatched canopy that provides ungulates and bears alike with shade and relief from insects during warmer months. Willows provide great forage for moose, and where moose go bears are sure to follow. Barren ground grizzlies prey on moose, muskox, and the calves of both species in addition to caribou.

HUNTING BARREN GROUND GRIZZLIES

Hunting barren ground grizzlies in the Territory of Nunavut means booking a spring hunt with an Eskimo or Native Canadian guide. The ideal time for such a hunt is when enough snow still remains that guides can pick up the tracks of big bears and follow them until their hunters get close enough to shoot. Traditional barren ground grizzly hunts are conducted from snowmobiles if there is enough snow or on foot if spring comes early and snow melts.

Hunting barren ground grizzlies in Alaska's Brooks Range, the barrens of the Arctic National Wildlife Refuge (ANWR), the Northwest Territories (NWT), or Nunavut is a task for the spotting scope, particularly during late summer hunts. Hunter and guide spend long hours visually picking apart the vast open landscape searching for bears near willow thickets and along rivers and streams. Several times while hunting in Alaska's Brooks range, I've kicked out bears from streamside willow thickets, both big boars and sows with cubs.

Once you spot a bear, you and your guide hightail it toward a suitable ambush spot. You'll need hip boots in some places, such as Nunavut, with its many lakes, rivers, streams, and bogs. (And be aware that slogging through bogs in hip boots can test your endurance and will, especially when you miss a mossy tussock and plunge into water deeper than the top of your boot.) Also pack plenty of moleskin, because navigating mossy stump tundra, where your feet bobble about incessantly and never seem to get a purchase on solid ground, usually turns into the "agony of da feet" after several days.

As you stalk closer, you and your guide must remain aware of the bear's keen sense of smell, its eyesight, and hearing, particularly as you travel through willows or water. Any time you approach a moving bear, whether it's traveling away from you or not, take nothing for granted. As you slip closer, the bear occasionally may disappear from sight, and at such times you will have no idea what it's doing. It might decide to change course and run straight for you, or it might spot prey nearby. Remember that over a short distance a grizzly is faster than a horse. When in grizzly country, always be prepared to shoot and shoot quickly.

Remaining hidden in the earth's folds or behind rocks is an excellent tactic to use when you attempt to slip closer to a bear. You can also remaining hidden as you sneak along a willow-

One way to approach an open-ground grizzly is to drop down within the banks of a creek to obscure your movements. (Credit: Kathy Etling)

covered bank or behind an esker snaking its way across a glacial plain. (An esker is a curving ridge made up of rock deposited eons ago by a stream that wound its way beneath a glacial ice sheet.) Another way to approach a grizzly is to partially or completely obscure your movements by dropping down within the banks of a creek or river channel. If the terrain is too flat for any of these tactics, wait until the bear obscures itself before attempting to move closer. When the animal lies down, enters the willows, moves behind an esker, or climbs down into a creek channel, that is your cue to resume your stalk. Move whenever you are unable to see the bear's eyes. If the animal is foraging as it travels, wait until its head is turned away from you or until it seems totally engrossed in feeding before easing forward. Whenever the bear lifts or turns its head, drop back down and freeze low to the earth until it resumes its activity. Because bears' eyes face forward, as humans' do, their peripheral vision is unlikely to tip them off to your presence as long as you remain a reasonable distance away. If you are close to a bear, however, all bets are off.

Grizzly-bear hunters, like black-bear hunters, use a variety of items to check wind direction, including API's Windfloaters, unscented talcum or scent-check powder, or a cigarette-lighter's flame.

THE TERRITORY OF NUNAVUT

Barren ground grizzlies seem to be thriving in the new Canadian territory of Nunavut. Most Americans have no idea what Nunavut is, or where it's located, but here's a brief lesson on a government created on April 1, 1999, when a block of land was carved from the eastern portions of the Northwest Territories.

The Territory of Nunavut was proposed in a 1976 document submitted to the Canadian government by the Inuit peoples of the Northwest Territories. This document, the *Nunavut Proposal,* was written by tribal elders to settle the Inuit's long-standing claim to their traditional homeland. Today Nunavut is a territory, but one day Inuit leaders may press for full provincial status.

OTHER PLACES TO HUNT BARREN GROUND GRIZZLIES

Both Alaska and the Northwest Territories have limited barren ground grizzly tags available. (Although some people refer to Alaska's northernmost grizzly population as "barren ground" grizzlies, strictly speaking the bears probably should be termed mountain grizzlies.) Grizzlies in the NWT inhabit land from the tundra barrens above the northernmost tree line to the MacKenzie mountains in the west. Be careful if you hunt there. Arctic weather can be extremely unpredictable and cold spells and high winds may occur suddenly, without warning.

IF YOU GO BARREN GROUND GRIZZLY HUNTING . . .

The remoteness of the barren ground grizzly hunting areas and limited rescue capabilities increase the risk of many natural hazards. You must be prepared to deal with extreme and rapidly changing weather, unpredictable river crossings, high winds, and dangerous wildlife, including polar bears. If you book such a hunt be prepared to be fully responsible for your own life. Guides or outfitters can do only so much. In extreme circumstances, guides may be able only to take care of themselves. This means that saving your life may be up to you!

A COASTAL GRIZZLY BEAR HUNT

In 1997 Stan Godfrey, of the Pope and Young Club, experienced the hunt of a lifetime. Stan was bowhunting for grizzly bear in the Unalakleet River drainages in western Alaska with guides Vance Grishkowsky and Ron Sherer. Stan's hunting partner, Dan Brockman, was also bowhunting the big animals. The two archers were positioned in treestands near active bear feeding sites along the river's shoreline. These sites were scouted out each morning by guides who plied the nearby streams in jetboats.

On day six of Stan's hunt he watched rather disconsolately as a large bear walk past his stand thirty-two yards away. "It was a little too far for me to shoot and feel comfortable about it," Stan said. "I did not want to wound a grizzly, which would put me and my guide in a potentially dangerous situation when we later had to track it into the brush."

Stan knew this bear might have been the best opportunity he'd had. "Just then, I heard a loud splash," he said. "I slowly turned my head to see an equally large bear

Beautiful brown bear boars like this one killed by Jim Zumbo can be hunted along the coastlines of Alaska and British Columbia. (Courtesy: Jim Zumbo)

carrying a freshly caught salmon onto a nearby island in the river." The bear gobbled down the salmon, then started walking toward the man. "I could hear a riverboat approaching," Stan said. "But the bear kept coming."

The bear forded the shallow water between the island and the shore and then walked past Stan at a distance of eighteen yards. The bowhunter released the arrow and watched it enter the bear's body behind the animal's front leg. The bear roared, spun to bite at the spot where the arrow had penetrated, then walked back the way it had come. When the animal was about thirty yards away, it appeared to topple over in some sparse brush.

"When my guide finally arrived, I told him where I thought the bear had fallen," Stan said. "We slowly approached to find the grizzly dead in its tracks, thirty yards from where I had shot it."

The Alaska Department of Fish and Game aged the old boar at twenty-eight years. Its skull officially scored 24 4/16 Pope and Young points, ranking it among the top three grizzly bear trophies ever taken by an archer.

Merely considering a hunt in which you would pit yourself against the King of the Forest can get your heart thumping, but to score on a bear the equal of Stan Godfrey's seems the stuff of dreams, whether you're toting a .416 Rigby or a seventy-pound bow.

Rifle hunting for grizzlies and brown bears along the Alaskan and British Columbian coastlines relies heavily upon spot-and-stalk tactics. Even Stan Godfrey's success was highly dependent on his guides being able to take him to an area where bears were actively feeding. When you are constrained by time, remaining aware of bear movements is often an essential component of eventual success.

GRIZZLIES AND BAITING

Baiting is not permitted anywhere for grizzlies, although sometimes guides will set up close to the gut pile of a moose or caribou taken earlier in the season, perhaps by a previous client. Any gut pile that appears to have been claimed by a grizzly presents a prime opportunity for a hunter with a bear tag. If a bear has dragged a gut pile or carcass away and covered it with sticks and leaves, it will probably return to feed some more.

During springtime hunts, guides and clients usually direct their spotting scopes toward south-facing slopes, where grizzly bears congregate to graze on the first green growth of the season.

MOUNTAIN GRIZZLIES

During late summer and early fall, grizzlies may be found in open meadows foraging on berries. One hunter who capitalized on such a situation was Wisconsin's Chuck Schlindwein. "I believe in the American dream," Chuck said. "I hunt with a few doctors, but I never let that stop me even though they have way more money than I do. When they told me they were considering an Alaskan trip, I told them, 'Just give me a few years' notice and I'll go with you.' Three years ago they told me they were going to book with an outfitter. I began working every bit of overtime I could get." Chuck is a slate and tile roofer. It is a skilled profession, one that requires a lot of detail work, and one that is in great demand. As Chuck and his buddies set about the task of choosing an outfitter, they split up the outfitters' lists of references and called every single person that appeared on them.

After hearing nothing but glowing reports on outfitter Curly Warren, of Alaska's Stoney River Outfitters, their minds were made up. "We booked three years ahead," Chuck said.

The hunters anxiously awaited their Alaskan trip. When they finally flew into Stoney River Lodge, they were seriously stoked for their hunt. "After we flew in to Stoney River Lodge, we split up," said Chuck. "A pilot loaded me and my gear in a Super Cub and flew me thirty-seven miles north to where my guide was waiting at spike camp.

"I was mainly hunting moose, although Curly had mentioned that there were good numbers of grizzlies, too. Once we started hunting, we'd get up before light, drink hot coffee, and prepare some freeze-dried food inside the dome tent, then wait until light before leaving the tent. The tent had been set up in a real brushy area to protect us from the wind. We waited for light because we weren't eager to accidentally bump into any bears. Downslope was a big marshy area, which was ideal, since I really wanted a big moose."

The September sun in Alaska rises above the horizon and then remains there for hours. Chuck and his guide settled down where they could watch the swampy area downslope of the tent. In the middle of the bog, there was a big, grassy meadow. As the hunters glassed, they spotted movement to the left of this meadow. "The sun was in our eyes, but we finally decided that the movement was a grizzly feeding on blueberries. I'd purchased a grizzly tag almost as an afterthought, even though the guide had wanted me to buy a second caribou license," Chuck said. "I was interested in grizzlies because I'd never seen one in the wild.

"As we were watching the first bear, a second grizzly came out. I told the guide I saw another grizzly, but he didn't believe me. At about that time the first grizzly saw the second bear and stood up. The second, smaller grizzly started to run, and the first grizzly chased it. Both bears disappeared over the hill.

"My guide continued to blow on his moose call," Chuck said. "The smaller grizzly finally emerged directly below where we were waiting. It walked, stopped, looked back over its shoulder, and then walked some more. It came about 150 yards toward us, stopped, glanced back over its shoulder, and then entered the brush to our left.

"I then saw the big grizzly, farther behind but definitely following the smaller bear. It moved slowly along the same creek where the smaller animal had walked, occasionally 'whuffing.' When it whuffed, the hair stood up on the back of my neck. The bear continued to wander back and forth four or five hundred yards below us. The guide kept saying, 'He is a big bear.'

"'Maybe that bear is looking to be shot,' I finally said. My guide said, 'That's all I need to hear.' We got up and started walking through the brush toward the grizzly. The guide said, 'Chamber a round.' I said, 'Why? The bear is still four hundred yards away.' The guide replied, 'If we bump into that smaller bear, the big bear will charge. If he does, it will be a false charge. Try to stand your ground, but remember I'll be backing you up.'

"We kept walking, and the guide said that if the bear looked up, I should stop moving. He explained that he didn't think grizzlies could see all that well, but that they could distinguish movement. At about that time, the bear looked up. I stopped, but the guide didn't. The bear saw the guide's movement, and here he comes. He jumped the creek and rushed toward us.

Hunters spot for mountain grizzlies as the animals forage in open meadows for marmots or grubs. (Courtesy: Jim Zumbo)

"The guide said, 'Where is he?' I pointed toward the grizzly. The guide said, 'Whenever you want him, take him.'

"I dropped down on one knee, shot once, and the bear began biting where I'd shot him. The guide said, 'Shoot him again.' I thought my shot had been good, but I shot again. The bear now moved to the side a bit, then looked away. The guide said, 'Shoot him again.' I said, 'All I can see is his rear end.' The guide said, 'Then shoot him in the butt.' I did, and the bear fell. My first shot, though, was a killing shot. It had taken out both the animal's lungs."

Chuck was using a Browning A-bolt Stainless Stalker chambered for .30-06 Springfield. His ammunition was Federal's Hi-Energy 180-grain Nosler Partition loads. "On several occasions our guide said he liked the way Nosler partitions performed on moose and bear," Chuck said.

Chuck Schindlein bagged his grizzly on the first day he hunted in Alaska. He later learned that his grizzly qualified for Boone and Crockett's all-time records book with a skull measurement of 24 11/16 inches. Four or five days later, he bagged a massive 64 1/2-inch Alaska moose that missed qualifying for the all-time

Boone and Crockett record book by about an inch. Two days after the moose, Chuck shot a nice black bear.

CALLING GRIZZLIES

No guide seems willing to intentionally try to call grizzlies to the gun or bow. This tactic can get out of hand even when used for black bears, so that may explain their reluctance to experiment with grizzly calling. Nevertheless, many tales are told of hunters grunting for moose and getting the living daylights scared out of them by charging grizzlies.

Calling grizzlies would probably work—and work well—if guides and hunters were able to set up someplace where the bear could not take them by surprise. Hunters would have to be very aware and extremely brave to attempt to call in grizzlies in prime grizzly-bear range, but if they wanted to try it, the ideal call would be that of a moose. Especially effective would be a moose or elk calf in distress.

Mike Fejes, who has killed six Alaska brown bears, said that using a moose grunt call is a great way to find out if any bears are hiding near a gut pile or carcass cache. "Just call before you get too close," Mike said. "If bears are nearby they should stand up so you can see them." But don't attempt such a foolhardy tactic unless you're ready for the consequences, you can see in all directions for a great distance, or you are backed up by someone you trust who carries a big, accurate rifle.

MOUNTAIN GRIZZLIES

A grizzly bear living in the mountains and traveling along a trail often reaches out with the front paw that's nearest a tree and takes a swipe at it—a side swipe. To do this, the bear stands on its other three legs, and the claw mark on the tree is horizontal. No one knows what side swiping means, although it might be a loose territorial marker or simply a means of communicating the bear's presence to other local bears.

Grizzlies are also known for biting prominent trees within their range. These bite marks may mark an area as "belonging" to a particular bear or advertise the bear's size to other local bears. Hunters who knows their stuff can use the marks of canine teeth to arrive at an estimated size for the grizzly. The distance between the canine tooth centers reveals how far apart those teeth are. Larger bears' canine teeth, as you would guess, are farther apart than those of smaller bears.

My good friend Jim Zumbo, who is skilled at hunting every species of North American big game, was hunting grizzlies in Alaska during the 2002 spring season. "It was miserable," Jim said. "Rotten weather every day. I slept cold, ate cold, and was wet every minute of the day. I didn't have dry feet for ten days.

"We were grizzly hunting not far from Aniak, along the Kufko-Quim River," Jim continued. "It was darned good hunting. We'd see three or four grizzlies every day from camp. The mountains we were hunting were full of nasty alder thickets on

Hunters spot for mountain grizzlies as the animals forage in open meadows for marmots or grubs. (Courtesy: Jim Zumbo)

the lower slopes. Those alders just ripped and tore at you. Above this alder tangle, the mountains looked a lot like golf greens. Low bush blueberries grew everywhere. In springtime, the bears graze on the grass growing on these slopes.

"We'd seen a big griz across the river from our camp. It was brown with gray ears, so I think it was real old. Neither my guide nor I wanted to cross the river and get wetter, so we concentrated instead on a nice grizzly feeding on the open slope of the mountain behind camp. A grizzly in that scrub looks immense. There's no way you should lose it. Right before we left, we could see it about a mile away and upslope. We started climbing, dipped down to ford a small stream, and darned if we didn't lose sight of that bear.

"We continued climbing another quarter mile," Jim said. "As we were going up the trail, the bear was coming down the same trail. We saw each other at about twenty-five feet. The bear stood up on its hind legs when he saw us, and from where I stood he seemed about twenty-seven feet tall. An alder bush was in my way so I couldn't shoot. The bear rushed off the trail, ran a few yards away, popped his teeth,

Montana's Mike McDonald traveled to Alaska to bag this high-scoring Boone and Crockett grizzly bear. (Courtesy: Mike McDonald)

and stood up again to stare at us at about sixty or seventy yards. I settled the crosshairs on the center of his chest and slowly squeezed the trigger of my .338 Rem Ultra Mag. The bear went down, then clambered back to its feet and ran about eighty yards. It then dropped fell over and died.

"I was using Remington ammunition," Jim said. "Those Swift A-Frame 250-grain bullets really did some damage. What a bear-killing load!" Jim's grizzly squared out to seven and a half feet. The beautiful bear's pelt was a rich auburn brown. Jim had scored on just the second day of a ten-day hunt.

"The next day we went moose hunting," Jim said. "In that country that meant climbing up to this one ridge where we'd glass, and then glass some more. Glassing was all we wanted to do, too. Venturing into that valley full of alders would be like going straight into hell. You wouldn't do it unless there was a reward.

"That morning, Dwight Van Brunt, of Kimber Rifles, said he thought he saw a black bear. Well, my ears perked up. I would have liked to take another black bear. We started stalking it, but as we got closer the 'black' bear started coming toward us. It wasn't a black bear at all, but a monster grizzly. This big griz walked past us at thirty yards. As nice as the bear was I'd shot the day before, this one was better. It would have squared nine feet if it had squared an inch."

HUNTING BROWN BEARS

A brown bear is in a class by itself. Mature brown bear boars are usually quite large, and some are even huge. Brownies are intelligent and cunning, and they possess unbelievable strength. Most are shy, but every brown bear has the potential to be dangerous. Some brownies can be vindictive, and a few have even been reported to plan and enact methods of revenge! In short, brown bears may be more like humans than many of us would care to admit.

Brown bears have been placed high upon a pedestal by hunters who wonder what it would be like to go one-on-one with such magnificent creatures. Since the dawn of time, humans have sought ways to test the limits of their courage. It is not so much bravery that motivates brown bear hunters, but rather respect and admiration for their quarry. Like Native Americans and Native Canadians of an earlier age, today's brown bear hunters seek out the mightiest animal adversaries, not to diminish them by the animals' deaths, but to exalt these bears as opponents worthy of the near fortune

A brown bear is intelligent, cunning, and possesses a strength beyond belief. (Courtesy: Bob Beaulieu)

the hunters must spend to hunt them, the preparations and bad weather they must endure, and the endless introspection that commences as soon as their quest begins: *Why am I doing this? What do I hope to discover about myself? What if I fall short?*

Like the earliest humans, modern hunters are filled with awe at the prospect of walking upon the same terrain as these mighty bears. They are willing to gamble a lot of money for just a chance to see, and possibly kill, a big brown bear. They fly out in small airplanes that rumble to precarious stops along rocky streambeds and sometimes even flip over on sodden, sandy shorelines. Would-be brown bear hunters sometimes wind up hunting from these crippled planes, biding their time until they're rescued.

Weather looms as a possible impediment at almost every moment of the trip. Brown bear hunters far too often see their chances for a bear disappear amid fogs that cover brown bear country for days on end—fog so pea-soup thick that they render even the finest optics unusable. Brown bear hunters may spend an entire hunt in a tent buffeted by high winds and lashed by rain or snow. They must be ready, willing, and able to get wet, sleep cold, slog over long distances—sometimes on snowshoes—and be scared out of their wits by the sometimes-lunatic maneuvers of bush pilots. And always, as they slip cautiously through boggy thickets, clamber over small knolls, or stumble through the willows, they must be prepared to stare Death in its face without flinching.

A brown bear is tenacious. Its will to live is extreme. A brownie whose adrenaline is surging can keep going and going and going, even as shot after shot pierces its vitals. It is the brownie's ability to take and mete out abuse in equal measure that keeps so many big game hunters permanently enthralled by these tremendous carnivores.

Could any other hunting experience compare with the sight of an eleven-foot Alaska brown bear standing erect twenty yards in front of you, its five-inch-long ivory claws curling downward from front paws the width of serving trays? The bear is big enough. It is close enough. You know your weapon intimately. Your guide is ready to back you up. It is, in fact, the moment of truth.

Are you up to it?

Or not? For that is what brown bear hunting is all about, isn't it? Wondering if you will measure up against this magnificent creature. Wondering if, when the chips are down, you are up to the task as so many others have been.

The ones who weren't, well, they didn't live to talk about it. And if they did live, most returned to civilization strangely mute about their experiences. Such is the power of the bear to make you put up or shut up. Talk about *Fear Factor!*

And yet as big and as strong and as courageous as brown bears are, most will go out of their way to avoid people. As formidable as they appear, at least to us puny-by-comparison humans, brown bears will back down from a confrontation with one of us more often than not.

Yet there's always that element of unpredictability when one is hunting brown bears. That "What is it going to do next?" question that is never completely answered until you see it unfold with your own eyes.

A BROWN BEAR HUNTING TALE

My good friend Marlin Grasser, now retired, was an Alaskan Master Guide for fifty years. Marlin lived in Alaska from the time he was seventeen. He hunted big game all over the state, from the Brooks Range far up north to the Wrangells in the south to the Alaskan Peninsula far out west.

Marlin reminds me of a big brown bear himself: fearless, tough, and dogged in his determination. Unlike the brown bear, though, Marlin never backs down from anyone or anything. When one day he came across a set of huge bear tracks in the snow, Marlin and some other men followed them. The bear went up hills and down for more than three hours. It traversed alder patches and creek beds, but always managed to stay out of sight. When the men emerged from one particularly dense thicket, Marlin spotted the huge animal. "It was looking back at us over its shoulder from five or six hundred yards away," Marlin said. "Then it entered another brushy pocket. I told the hunter I'd go in after it and try to push it out the other side."

Remember that part about brown bears being cunning? Some really are. Unfortunately for Marlin, this was one of them. "The bear just wouldn't be pushed," he said. "I crept through the alders, but the bear remained in the thicket. I wasn't worried. I climbed in there with it because a bear will almost always run out the other side. If it had, my hunter would have a shot.

"The bear sat tight. I finally climbed up this one bank and spotted it sitting in a ring of tall grass. As soon as it spotted me, it charged. I was carrying an old Model 70 Winchester chambered in .300 H&H Magnum. The bear was coming so fast I had to shoot from my hip. The bullet tore into the bear. It fell down in front of me and lay there. I chambered another round and shoved the rifle barrel right against its back and pulled the trigger. Nothing happened. I ejected that round, chambered another, and did it again. All in all, I chambered three rounds and tried to fire them all, but the gun was broken."

At the sound of the last trigger click, the bear was up off the ground and all over Marlin. Marlin shoved the rifle into the animal's face, and it bit the stock and the barrel, which pushed it back a little. Brown bears and grizzlies usually go for the face, and this one was no exception. "It used its paw to slap the rifle out of my hand," Marlin explained. "The force knocked me over. When I flipped down on my back, my legs flew up into the air. The bear grabbed one of my legs with its teeth and bit it hard six or seven times. Then it growled and ran away."

Marlin's leg was ripped to pieces. Two puncture wounds had penetrated his shinbone and blood and marrow were oozing out. Marlin finally raised his head and saw that the bear's track leaving the area was full of blood.

"I got up and checked my gun," Marlin said. "A tag alder seed had somehow fouled up the firing pin. I cleaned the seed off so that it would shoot, and then I went after the bear. I tracked it to within thirty or forty yards of where my hunter was waiting.

"Didn't you hear that commotion?" I asked the man. "Oh, yes," he said. "I heard you shoot, and then I heard all the racket, but I didn't know you needed me."

Marlin figured that his hunter was just about useless. He told him to follow their tracks back to the hunting lodge and tell Marlin's son to send their pilot to help

Marlin locate the bear from above. Marlin then left the hunter as he gave chase to the wounded bear.

"I had quite a bit on my mind at that time," Marlin said. "But my hunter would have given me even more to think about. He went back to the lodge and told my son Eddie that a bear had mauled me and that I was dead. Then he cracked open a bottle of Seagram's Seven and started drinking. When the very next plane landed at our airstrip, my hunter boarded. I never heard from him again."

Marlin was badly wounded but determined to kill the bear. When the lodge's pilot flew low over him later that day, Marlin yelled to him, asking if he could see the bear. The pilot yelled back that the bear was at the top of the next alder patch.

"I climbed up, and sure enough, there's the bear, about sixty yards away," Marlin said. "As soon as he saw me, he charged. He just flew at me with his hind legs lunging. He was really moving, and I raised my gun and shot. The bear fell, scrambled up, and I shot again. It just kept running down the hill and across a creek."

Marlin had one shell left. "I waited a while, hoping it would give the bear time to die," he said. "Then I followed it. I walked down the hill and across the creek, and I cut another bear track. This one wasn't bloody. *Oh, hell,* I remember thinking. *Another bear. That's all I need.* I was pretty worried. I walked up and down the creek, looking. I stopped on a little knoll, and as I was standing there the bear walked out of an alder patch about sixty feet away. I hollered at him, "Hey, bear!" The bear turned, looked at me, and charged. I shot again. The last bullet I had with me. This bullet went in his back just behind the shoulder and dropped him. I sat there on the ground for a good long time before I gathered the courage to see if he was really dead."

BROWN BEAR HUNTING METHODS

STALKING BROWN BEARS IN SOUTHEAST ALASKA'S COASTAL RAINFOREST

Alaska brown bears *(Ursus arctos middendorffi)* are hunted both spring and fall, depending on where you plan to hunt. In the spring bears are scattered on side hills after they emerge from their dens. They forage for tender grasses and also sedges near the edges of lakes and streams. The claws of spring bears are longer than at any other time of the year, and their hides are often very nice, too.

In the fall, brown bears concentrate near stream tributaries, where they fish for salmon to gain as much weight as possible before winter sets in.

Many brown bear outfitters hunt their clients out of boats or motorized rafts. Guides and hunters glass the shoreline or tidal flats searching for foraging brown bears. Some also climb hills where they can spot for long distances. When a suitable bear is located, the boat is beached or the hunters simply stalk as close as possible before shooting.

Another way to hunt these bears is to fly over the coast, searching for a big brownie feeding on a kill. If a bear is located actively feeding, there is a good chance it will still be near the kill when hunters return on foot the next day. (In Alaska it is illegal to fly—other than in a commercial airliner—and hunt bears in the same day.)

THE ALASKA PENINSULA: The Alaska Peninsula has been designated a "trophy bear area" since 1976 to ensure the quality of these giant bears for years to come. When this area was first designated Alaska wildlife officials decided that spring hunts would take place in even-numbered years and fall hunts would occur in odd-numbered years. The only North American hunt

Many outfitters and guides conduct their bear hunts from boats like this one. (M. R. James photo)

more costly than an Alaska brown bear hunt is a polar bear hunt, and a polar bear hunt isn't much more expensive.

Senior airman Theodore Winnen, a load crew member with the 18th Fighter Squadron, Eielson Air Force Base, decided during mid-October, 2001, to go Sitka blacktail hunting with his buddy, Staff Sgt. Jim Urban, and two other friends. Their destination: Hitchenbrook Island in the Gulf of Alaska's Prince Edward Sound. Many stories have been circulated about Winnen's big bear. In fact, within a few weeks' of the animal's encounter with the airman the bear had "grown" in myth to an almost unbelievable 12-feet 6-inches in stature and over 1,800 pounds in weight, neither of which were true.

Winnen and three hunting buddies were dropped off on Hinchenbrook by an air taxi on the morning of October 14. Hinchenbrook, a mere 165-square miles in size, harbors about one hundred Alaska brown bears, a density that is higher than on any other island in the Sound, according to Cordova area wildlife biologist Dave Crowley, who works for the state's department of fish and game.

Winnen had purchased a bear hunting permit just in case he happened to encounter one of the huge bears for which the Alaskan coastal islands are so famous. As the skies cleared on the morning of October 15, Winnen and Urban started hunting. The two men followed a creek bed upstream as they searched for deer. Urban was armed with a .300-caliber Win. Mag., while Winnen carried a .338 Win. Mag. As the hunters walked farther up the creek they noticed a pool full of dying salmon. Both men knew such a scene would be highly appealing to a hungry bear. The two men continued following the creek upstream until they came to a small island ringed with thick brush. Some blueberries still clung to their bushes. On the island grew a huge spruce tree and at its base was what looked to be the start of a large hole.

At about 9:30 A.M., Winnen glanced upstream to see a big brown bear just forty yards away. The bear was flipping over logs looking for salmon.

"He's a shooter," Urban whispered. Both men jacked shells into their guns, then took off their packs and laid them at the base of the huge spruce which was nearby. They then moved a few feet farther upstream. Winnen scanned the small amount of real estate between the two men and the bear. He noticed a large tree that had fallen to the ground, and told Urban, "When the bear crawls over that log we'll take him."

The only problem was that the bear moved so fluidly over the log, as if it had not even been there, that neither hunter was able to get off a shot.

As the bear continued down the creek, the two hunters lost sight of him. They retreated to the big spruce where they had left their packs. As they waited there, a few seconds later the bear appeared just ten yards in front of them. "He was coming toward us," Winnen said. Winnen tried to aim for the bear's chest, but all he could see through his scope was the bear's head. Urban said, "Shoot! Shoot!"

Winnen recalled aiming for the bear's left eye. The bullet, however, hit two inches lower, entering the side of the bear's muzzle and entering its brain. Winnen continued to shoot. All in all, he fired six shots into the big brownie.

In photos, the bear's paw is almost as wide as the hunter's chest and sports three- to four-inch claws. Winnen guessed the bear's hide weighed more than 200 pounds.

Once back at the base, Winnen took the hide and skull to the state Department of Fish and Game to get it sealed, as required by law. Fish and Game records reveal the skull's unofficial Boone and Crockett green score of 28 and 8/16 inches, while the hide squared 10-feet, 6-inches. Biologist Crowley said he suspects the bear was 15 to 20 years old. Based on the bear's girth measurement it is estimated that the bear weighed somewhere between 1,000 and 1,200 pounds, far larger than almost any other bear ever taken on Hichenbrook Island.

THE KENAI PENINSULA: The Kenai Peninsula in south central Alaska is connected to the rest of the state by a narrow, heavily glaciated corridor. Few bears migrate through this corridor, making the Kenai brown bear population essentially a closed group.

Bob Fromme used his bow to take this big British Columbia grizzly in 2000. The bear's skull scored 24 4/6 using the Pope and Young system. (Courtesy: Bob Fromme)

Alaska Department of Fish and Game biologists estimate that somewhat more than three hundred brown bears inhabit this area, with well over half that number found in the peninsula's western portion. One hundred or more brownies inhabit the peninsula's eastern edge along the Gulf of Alaska and farther north.

THE ABC ISLANDS: Admiralty, Baranof, and Chicagof Islands support large brown bear populations. Admiralty holds more than 1700 bears, while Baranof supports more than one thousand of the animals. Chicagof is home to almost 1800 brownies. Kruzof, a smaller island in the same archipelago, has a population of about 125 brown bears. The island with the greatest density of brown bears is Admiralty, where 386 bears can be found on every one thousand square kilometers.

HUNTING KODIAK BROWN BEARS

The name says it all: Kodiak! Any bear hunter, including those who have not yet hunted these animals but would like to, knows that Kodiak brownies are, if not the largest carnivorous land mammal, then among the largest. Some bear hunters believe—and California's Mike Fejes is one of them—that Unimak Island's brown bears are somewhat larger than Kodiak's.

The Alaska Department of Fish and Game, though, votes for the Kodiak. According to Larry Van Daele, biologist in charge of Kodiak Island, "Kodiak bears are the largest bears in the world. A large male can be over ten feet tall when standing on his hind legs and five feet tall at the top of his hump when he is standing on all four legs. A large boar will weigh as much as fifteen hundred pounds." As is always the case, hunters and outfitters tell of unsubstantiated records of bears weighing even more.

BOB FROMME'S KODIAK HUNT

Kodiak browns of almost any size, though, are large enough to attract the attention of any serious bear hunter. One such hunter was archer Bob Fromme of San Diego, California. Fromme had been wanting for years to take one of the giants with a bow. He'd booked and gone on a number of combination hunts for caribou and other game that also would have allowed him to shoot a brown bear by paying an additional trophy fee. Fromme never saw a bear on any of these hunts, so he went for broke and booked a hunt with Tom Kirstein, a guide from Fairbanks.

"Timing on any brown bear hunt is critical," Fromme said. "Hunters think of hunting brown bears while they are fishing for salmon like the photos depict from the McNeil River Wildlife Refuge. That may seem ideal, but it isn't reality for anyone hoping to kill a Kodiak brown bear.

"The salmon run from around August 1 to October 1," Fromme continued. "That is an excellent time to hunt brown bears in the Alaskan Peninsula, where hunting season corresponds fairly well with the salmon run.

"On Kodiak, though, the fall season doesn't start until the last week of October, when salmon runs are finished. The spring Kodiak bear hunting season is a month long. It begins on April 15 and ends May 15. Outfitters book hunters on fifteen-day hunts, so you have a choice of hunting from April 15 to April 30 or from May 1 to May 15. Hunters who go during the earlier period have the best chance of taking a boar whose coat is not yet rubbed, but these hunters may not see many bears if spring is late and the animals remain in their dens. Another downside to the earlier hunt occurs when snow still covers the earth. It is quite strenuous to hike around in deep snow and even harder to stalk a bear in it. The later spring hunt, from May 1 to May 15, guarantees hunters that more bears will be out, although many of them will be sows and cubs. The chance that you will have to contend with deep snow lessens as well on a later hunt."

Fromme's outfitter had his clients hunt Kodiak's fabled Deadman Bay area. Fromme's plane was unable to land at the Kodiak airport until the second day of his hunt—not uncommon on Alaskan hunting trips. Once they arrived in camp, Fromme's guide immediately hurried him to a boat for a quick trip across the bay to a spot where the guide knew big boars liked to den up for the winter.

"We set up high on one slope overlooking a large basin," Fromme said. "From where we were sitting I could see another slope, and that's where the boars liked to den." As the pair watched this slope, they spotted a big boar. Before they could move, though, a resident hunter killed the animal. Fromme wanted to move. "I can't stand hunting where someone else has just shot up the place," he noted.

Fromme and his guide returned to their boat. They set out and started glassing the shoreline. It didn't take long for the guide to spot some huge tracks in the snow. He noted how far apart the tracks were as well as the amount of drag. A giant of a boar will plow through some drifts rather than walking or leaping because the animal is so powerful that bulling its way through snow does not even faze it.

"The guide suspected we were looking at a huge boar's tracks," Fromme said. "We could see where the trail disappeared into the island's interior. The time was 8:30 P.M. I knew it would be getting dark at 10 P.M. We waited for a while, and when the bear didn't reappear, I decided to sneak along his trail to see if I could spot him.

"He was feeding in a thick patch of alders only about a hundred yards from his trail along the shoreline," Fromme said. "As I tried to move closer, he must have spotted my movement and spooked somewhat. I roared at him, trying to calm him down by making him think my movement was made by another bear. Then I hit a rabbit call, thinking that might help calm him, too, if not bring him out to investigate the sound. He didn't bolt out of the thicket, so we decided to let him settle down for about fifteen minutes or so before I attempted to go any closer."

Fromme's guide was worried about the amount of remaining daylight. He wondered

Bowhunter Bob Fromme stalked into an alder thicket with this big Kodiak brown to shoot it from eighteen yards. (Courtesy: Bob Fromme)

if there was enough time for Fromme to get off a shot before dark no matter what action he decided on. After the fifteen-minute wait was up, Fromme took off his outermost boot layer. The outfitter had advised his hunters to cut down a pair of neoprene stocking-foot chest waders and wear them inside a pair of ordinary hunting or hiking boots to act as hip boots when crossing creeks or bogs. The hunters wore them rolled down for normal walking and pulled them up thigh-high when they negotiated water hazards.

"Once my hiking boots were off, I pulled up the hip boots and then knelt down in the snow and mud," Fromme said. "I don't know if I'd have gotten away with this if the boar hadn't been groggy after having just left his winter den. I'd sneak closer to him on my knees for about two minutes—about that time he'd lift his head and look around. I'd stop whenever he was watching and then sneak forward again. I was about forty yards away when he rolled over on his side. This gave me the chance I'd been waiting for. He wouldn't be able to see me move, so I stood up and tippy-toed around him from the rear. There was a jungle of alders behind where he was lying, but also a stream. My goal was to make it to a spot with the right angle, so my arrow could take out both of his lungs. I crept closer and closer until I was twenty-one yards from him. Only a bush blocked my shot. I took a couple more steps to get around the bush and was now eighteen yards from this huge boar.

"I had paid for a cameraman to accompany me so he could videotape my bear hunt," Fromme continued. "The cameraman saw how close I was to the bear, and he remarked that if the bear tried to jump me, the guide would not have a good shot at the animal. So the guide began to move closer. He took a couple of steps, and the bear must have suspected something was up, because he pulled his front legs up so that his front end was off the ground. The way he stopped gave me a perfect triangle behind his front legs to aim at. I released, and my arrow hit him in his right side. It went all the way through his body, and the broadhead and six inches of arrow shaft were sticking out on the other side. He felt the pain, bit at his side where the arrow had gone in, and grunted. The he turned around. I knew he would probably run toward me because I was on the thick side of the alder patch, and he did. I froze until he was about ten yards away, and then I backed up a little. He headed up higher through the alders, but he couldn't go far. He rolled over and died. Only about eight seconds had elapsed from the moment I shot until the bear died."

Bob Fromme killed his Kodiak brown bear in May 2002. The hide squared ten feet four and one-half inches, and the skull's Pope and Young green score was 28 8/16 points. Although not yet officially scored after the drying period, Fromme's bear's green score exceeds the official Pope and Young score of the current record, which was taken by Jack Frost. Fred Bear's brown bear is the current number two brown bear in the world. An estimate of the bear's weight during the fall, when the animal would have been in peak condition, was fourteen hundred pounds.

Fromme was shooting a Mathews Rival Pro with a draw weight of seventy-five pounds and a draw length of thirty inches. He used Blackhawk Vapor All-Carbon arrows tipped with Rocket Ultimate STeel fixed-blade three-blade broadheads. This combination of arrow and broadhead weighed in at 500 grains and traveled at 260 feet per second. Fromme's bow was also fully equipped with Sims anti-vibration products, including dampeners and stabilizer. The archer wore Scent-Lok beneath his camouflage. The camouflage pattern he selected was Bill Jordan's Timber Advantage.

Kodiak brown bears *(Ursus arctos middendorffi)* are a unique subspecies of the brown or grizzly bear. They live exclusively on the islands in the Kodiak Archipelago, where they have been isolated from other brown bears for about twelve thousand years.

Today between 2,800 and 3,000 bears inhabit Kodiak Island at a density of about 0.7 bears per square mile. Kodiak bear populations are healthy, and they enjoy a relatively pristine habitat and well-managed fish populations.

Kodiak Numbers

Even though Kodiak bear numbers are stable, and in some places are increasing, a major mortality factor for Kodiak cubs is cannibalism by adult male bears. Mature boars may not only kill and eat cubs, but they also occasionally kill a mature sow simply because she is not in estrus. There is no way of knowing how such behaviors affect overall bear numbers, but there is little doubt that having hunters kill mature boars helps ensure that more young bears will survive to adulthood. Even so, over twenty-five percent of Kodiak cubs die before striking out on their own.

Kodiak brown bear sows become sexually mature at the age of five and continue throughout their lives to produce cubs. Usually four years elapse between litters, so recruitment is low, one reason cub cannibalism is of such concern. Litters consist of only two or three cubs, although a sow occasionally may be seen with five or six tagging along behind her. Biologists suspect that such sows have adopted orphaned cubs to raise as their own.

BOB BEAULIEU'S KODIAK HUNT

All facets of the brown bear's life are fascinating, especially to those who hunt them. No wonder people are so willing to pay almost a king's ransom to line up their sights on one of these immense beasts. One who did just that was Bob Beaulieu. Although Bob had retired before he went brown bear hunting in April 2000, he never gave up on his dream of someday hunting the giant brownies.

Using a rather roundabout method of research, Bob found a master guide, Jim Bailey, of Eagle River, Alaska, who had had a cancellation for April. That truly was fortuitous, considering that most brown bear hunts are booked five years in advance.

Bob and his wife traveled from their Florida home to Kodiak, Alaska. "I hunted fairly early in the year," Bob said, "when the whole idea is to glass the hillsides looking for big bears and hope you see enough bears to make a good selection. Jim boated us to an area about an hour from Kodiak. We were put up fairly luxuriously, in shacks rather than tents. The weather didn't cooperate at all. I hunted for three days, and there was only one afternoon when it wasn't raining, snowing, or sleeting.

"The snowline where we hunted that afternoon [I shot the bear] was at about a thousand feet," Bob continued. "When we finally started to glass, we spotted a sow with a cub and another bear with a pretty substantial rub spot.

"My guide was young, but he was a very good guide," Bob said. "We spent a lot of time glassing the snowline, where bear tracks were clearly visible. One set had tracks so big it looked like a truck had made them. When the guide spotted these big tracks, we crawled up closer to them and started spotting from there. It was rough going. The snow was waist-deep in places. I'd taped my gun barrel so I could be certain it would shoot. I was more concerned about my scope, because I had used the gun as a walking stick when it was difficult to negotiate in the snow.

"Finally, we saw a bear about two miles away," Bob said. "It was the first bear we'd seen. It would walk a while, then roll over on its back and play with its feet. The guide said it looked like a good bear, one that would measure at least eight feet. He also said we had to get ahead of it so I could get a shot at it.

"It took about an hour to get into position," Bob continued. "The bear was walking toward this deep ravine. We walked ahead of it and got onto the other side of that ravine and waited. Pretty soon we could see the bear coming toward us. I'd been winded, but had had time to catch my breath, and I was ready to shoot. The guide told me he'd stop the bear. He yelled once, then again, but the wind caught his words, and I know the bear hardly heard them, but he looked directly toward us anyway. A head-on shot was not what I was hoping for. The bear finally began to go down the ravine, and I was able to shoot it through the back." Bob's Winchester Model 70 (post-1994) was chambered for .375 H&H Mag. His ammunition was Federal's 300-grain Bear Claw Trophy Bonded Sledgehammer. A Nikon 3–7X variable was atop bob's rifle, mounted on see-through iron sights. When Bob's bullet struck the bear behind its shoulder at 150 yards, the bear immediately started shaking like its spine had been broken. "The recoil caused me to lose sight of the bear, and when I looked again, it was gone," Bob said. "I asked my guide, 'Where's the bear?' He said, 'It dropped like a rock. Keep shooting.' 'At what?' I said, because I was still unable to see the bear. I shot a few times in its direction, but to this day I'm not sure I hit it again."

Bob Beaulieu knew how lucky he'd been. Looking back, he knew he had about a one in five chance of making such a low-percentage stalk without blowing it. "Plus, this was the only bear we'd seen after several days of bad weather," Bob said. "I call it my once-in-a-lifetime bear."

Bob is right in more ways than one. His big Kodiak brown bear really was a once-in-a-lifetime bruin. His boar's skull measured 26 4/16 points using the Boone and Crockett scoring system, so the bear qualified for the club's annual awards dinner.

Although generally solitary in nature, Kodiak bears sometimes gather in large groups where there is an abundance of food. To avoid fights, especially between boars of disparate ranks that could easily be killed in such an altercation, Kodiak brown bears have developed a complex system of body language, facial expressions, and sounds to express their desires and to avoid battles.

Kodiak bears were commercially hunted throughout the 1800s. A bear hide brought only about ten dollars at the time, which is no more than what a beaver or river otter pelt was worth.

Farmers at one time tried to raise livestock on Kodiak Island, but bears promptly scrambled their efforts. They then began to systematically kill the big brownies, and bear numbers plunged. Sportsmen became so worried about the drop in bear numbers that they petitioned the federal government to protect both bears and their Kodiak habitats. As a result, the Kodiak National Wildlife Refuge was created in 1941.

Today hunters kill about 160 Kodiak bears annually. Regulations are strict. Each year about five thousand resident hunters apply for a chance at the 319 permits set aside for them. Nonresidents regard as more precious than gold any permit they receive. As of press time, to hunt Kodiak brown bears you need a valid Alaska hunting license, a Big Game Tag Record, a brown bear locking tag, and a registration and/or drawing permit for the area you plan to hunt. If you are not an Alaska resident, you also need proof that you will be guided by a registered guide or a relative within the second degree of kinship.

Registration permits are issued for those who hunt bears along Kodiak's road system. These permits can be obtained only at Kodiak's Alaska Department of Fish and Game office. They issue an unlimited number of registration permits, and the permits can be obtained by either residents or nonresidents.

Drawing permits are issued for bear hunting in all other parts of Game Management Unit 8 (Kodiak Archipelago). There are twenty-nine Drawing Hunt Areas, and the hunts are further divided by season and hunter residency, with a total of 472 permits issued annually. Most of these permits are issued to hunters selected in a lottery. A limited number are also available for nonresident clients of guides with exclusive use areas on the Kodiak National Wildlife Refuge.

Bear hunter success averages thirty-five percent for Alaska residents and seventy-five percent for guided nonresident hunters, with spring hunts having a slight advantage over fall hunts.

Trophy-class bears have been taken in nearly every drainage on Kodiak and Afognak Islands. During the last spring hunt for which Alaska officials have complete records, bears with skull sizes exceeding twenty-eight inches were killed in the following hunt areas: Halibut Bay, South Uyak Bay, Uganik Lake, Wild Creek, Aliulik Peninsula, South Arm of Uganik, and Deadman Bay.

HUNTING SIBERIAN BROWN BEARS

Warren Parker is a member of an exclusive club. Warren, a Missouri building contractor as well as the former president of Safari Club International, is one of the few people to have killed animals representing every legal, recognized bear species in the world. Warren's "World Bear Slam" includes an American black bear, an Alaska brown bear, a grizzly bear, a barren ground grizzly bear, a polar bear, an Amur bear, a European brown bear, a Mid-Asian brown bear, a Kamchatka brown bear, and a Siberian brown bear.

As you might expect, Warren experienced some thrilling moments as he collected

Warren Parker and his Siberian brown bear, which is part of his SCI World Bear Slam. (Courtesy: Warren Parker)

his Bear Slam. "My Siberian brown died at my feet," he remarked. "I was one of the first hunters ever allowed to hunt Yukitiz, east of the Lena River, in Russia. This was during the latter part of the 1980s. We were there in the fall to hunt snow sheep. I really didn't even know the area had any brown bears.

"My guide and I had spotted a small band of sheep up in the mountains," Warren continued. "We made a good stalk, but the sheep weren't what I was after. Luckily, as I'd stalked closer, I'd jacked a shell into the chamber of my rifle. To pull out of that country, we had to cross a small valley. We started across a small plateau and I could barely believe my eyes when I saw a big bear running right at me in a full charge."

Without thinking, Warren aimed and shot his .270 Win, which was loaded with a 130-grain bullet, hardly the load for an enraged bear. In short order, he delivered two quick shots through the bear's lungs.

"The bear started spinning, as bears often will when they're hit hard," Warren continued. "The animal forgot I was even there as he continued to spin rapidly just twelve inches from where I was standing. I finally put one last shot in the boar's skull to put him down for good."

Warren Parker's great Siberian brown bear was ranked number one in the world in SCI's record book for many years. The big boar squared eight feet and sported a lovely dark brown, silver-tipped coat.

Warren Parker's Kamchatka brown bear hunt came about almost by chance as well. Russia's Kamchatka Peninsula is across the Bering Sea from Alaska. "This hunt was an interesting deal, too," Warren commented. "I was there in autumn to hunt the Kamchatka sheep. I'd already bagged my ram, so my guide and I decided to drop down into the lowlands.

"When we arrived there, I couldn't believe what I was seeing," Warren continued. "We walked out upon this huge plateau—perhaps fifteen miles square—and there must have been at least a hundred bears on the plateau feeding on low bush blueberries. To take a bear, all a hunter would have to do would be to work the plateau's perimeter until he found a bear big enough to take, then stalk slowly toward the animal until he had a shot."

If only things had been that simple.

"I had a cameraman along to film my hunt," Warren said. "I admit I probably pushed the envelope too hard on this occasion. I tried to get too close to the bear I'd chosen. As I was standing there about a hundred yards from the bear, it turned around and immediately charged me. At that same moment, another big boar, this one about seventy-five yards away, charged me, too. I fired three shells at the one, reloaded, and then shot two bullets into the second.

"Both were simply outstanding animals," Warren concluded. "One squared eleven feet, while the other squared ten feet, six inches." Warren shot his two huge—and quite cranky—Kamchatka brown bears with a .300 Win Mag and 180-grain Nosler handloads.

POLAR BEAR NATURAL HISTORY

Polar bears, or Nanuq as they are called by the natives, are the great wanderers of the frozen north. Their home is a shifting, moving sheet of ice that buckles, gives, breaks off into floes, and delivers the great white bears to various parts of their worldwide polar haunts. The great bears wander hundreds of miles in the open leads of pack ice in a never-ending quest for food.

Polar bears are found off the northern North American coast, in northern Russia to Siberia, in Greenland, in Norway, and on other arctic islands to the southern limit of the pack ice.

The white bears are superb swimmers and can travel great distances in the icy polar seas. The animals swim in open leads with just their eyes and noses visible above the water's surface. As they approach seals lying on the ice, the great bears leap directly out of the water and onto the ice, where they grab the seals and kill them with a quick bite to the head or a cuff from a huge front paw.

They may also search for a seal's breathing hole and patiently wait for the animal to come up for air—or find a ringed seal's birthing chamber, break into it, and kill mother and young.

Polar bears usually don't consume the seal's meat, but dine on the animal's blubber. Arctic foxes are the beneficiaries of such picky eating habits. The smaller carnivores are often found eating the meat of seal kills left behind by the bears.

Polar bears are also known to devour walruses, and they will eat whales that flounder and die on the ice pack.

Polar bears can eat ten percent of their body weight in half an hour. After gorging on a seal, the bear may lie flat on its belly on the ice to try to cool its stomach.

The polar bear's coat is the very model of evolutionary adaptation. Although polar bears are very closely related to brown bears, it is difficult to tell this by merely looking at the two animals. Polar bears are white, sleek, and streamlined. They are masterful swimmers and true carnivores, except for females in the spring. (After denning and giving birth, females dine on sedges or grasses to blow their plugs. They then lead their young to the shores of the polar ice cap to await the day when they will once more take to the sea to hunt seals.)

The polar bear's long white coat is the key to its survival. Long guard hairs overlay a dense, downy underfur that mats in the same manner that wool felts to keep the bear warm and its skin dry. The long guard hairs also serve to trap heat from the sun.

Beneath the fur, polar bears' skin is black to retain heat. The combination of long, thick hair, dense, matted underfur, and black skin keeps the polar bear comfortable at temperatures approaching −100°F. Oil in the bears' thick coats makes them shed water as do a duck's feathers, so even when the bears plunge into the icy depths, they never feel uncomfortable. A four-inch layer of fat beneath the skin also aids their insensitivity to cold.

Polar bears' heads are tapered, with small ears and strong jaws. They appear ideally put together for swimming, with their sleek outlines and webbed paws, and they can swim a phenomenal sixty miles or more without resting. The bears' paws are platter-sized not only to improve swimming speed, but also to help stabilize them on slippery ice and distribute their great weight on sometimes fragile ice.

Adult males can weigh 1,600 pounds, and some animals may weigh even more. An average-sized female weighs about 550 pounds.

Polar bears are sexually mature at about five years of age, but most males do not mate until they are eight to ten years old. Males have the urge to mate, but older, stronger animals prevent younger males from attempting to breed.

Mating generally takes place during April and May, which is one reason hunts are scheduled during these months—with big bears roaming the ice to seek mates, the hunter's job is made easier.

Cubs are born in a snow den between November and January after a gestation period of between seven and eight months.

Male polar bears remain active during the long winter nights, when they remain out on the ice pack hunting for food.

Polar bears have been known to live for thirty years. Most bears in captivity live for sixteen to twenty years.

In the 1960s, the world's polar bear population was only about ten thousand animals. That inspired the United States, Canada, the Soviet Union, Norway, and Denmark in 1981 to sign an agreement limiting polar bear hunting. Today the population is estimated at about forty thousand bears, and the population is either stable or increasing slightly wherever the big animals are found.

Today subsistence hunters account for most polar bear kills. Alaska bars its natives from selling their permits to nonresident hunters. Other countries are not so strict; for example, income from polar bear hunters has become a vital part of the economy in Canada's Nunavut and Northwest Territories.

HUNTING POLAR BEARS

GLORIA ERICKSON'S HUNT

"Hunting polar bears in the traditional Inuit manner was the greatest experience of my life," said Gloria Erickson, a Nebraska farmer and hunter. "Before I went on my polar bear hunt I talked to half a dozen men who had gone on similar hunts. Most of them told me it was the worst experience they'd ever had. One said, 'It's going to be the toughest thing you've ever done. You'll have to be mentally prepared and mentally tough. You'll be cold all the time, you won't see much wildlife, you're away from your own culture, and then things will *really* get bad.' He finished by saying, 'And I hope you like the color white, because that is all you're going to see for weeks at a time.'

"How wrong he was," Gloria said. "The Arctic isn't all white, but shades of blue and green and gray. Pressure ridges formed by stresses on freezing sea water cause the ocean to assume such fantastic shapes, it's like hunting on the moon. I thought the polar landscape was truly gorgeous!

"And the Inuit are such wonderful people. When I was introduced at a meeting of the village elders, I explained, through an interpreter, that I was there to experience how they, the Inuit, have survived for thousands of years, although I'd be using a .416 Remington, and not a harpoon. They understood, and I think they liked hearing it. They are just like us. They enjoy being with people who have a genuine interest in them and what they do."

Gloria endured two days in an Arctic whiteout. On the sixth day of her hunt she told her guide that she wanted to kill only a big boar. "I did not want to kill a female, no matter what," she said. "We were riding along on the dogsled, and we suddenly cut this bear track. I knew when I saw it that it had been made by a big bear."

Gloria's Inuit guide led the sled dogs along the trail of fresh tracks. Several hours later, the guide and his hunter spotted the big bear standing on top of a pressure ridge. The guide released two of his dogs, which ran to the bear and began worrying the large carnivore as sled dogs have done for centuries when their masters have gone polar bear hunting. Gloria and her guide, meanwhile, took the dogsled to the other side of the pressure ridge. When she was finally in shooting position, Gloria found that the huge white bear was only thirty yards away. As she settled down, her guide leaped around on the ice, shouting, "Shoot him, shoot him!"

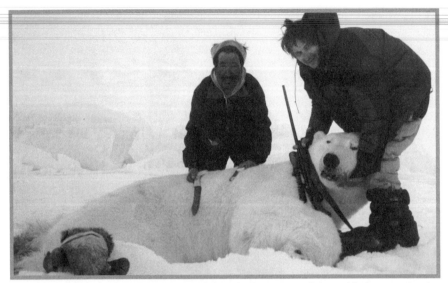

A traditional polar bear hunt for Nanuq, Inupiak for polar bear, is one of the world's last great hunting adventures. (Courtesy: Canada North Outfitters)

"I shot once, and the bear disappeared," Gloria recalled. "When we climbed over the pressure ridge, my bear was lying dead on the other side." Gloria's big bear, which is ranked very high in SCI's record book, missed qualifying for the *Boone and Crockett Records of North American Big Game* by a single point.

A HUNT FOR NANUQ

No matter how you look at it, a traditional polar bear hunt for Nanuq is one of the world's last great hunting adventures. Your hunt begins when you arrive in a Native Canadian village. You are introduced to your hosts and then fitted with the traditional Inuit hunter's outfit of green caribou skins that the natives tanned by urinating on them. Not a pleasant thought, perhaps, but such clothing keeps hunters warm no matter what the weather is. Just don't try to take this warm, traditional hunting clothing back home with you. The moment it thaws, the odors emanating from the skins will be memorable.

Some modern polar bear hunters prefer to bring their own high-tech clothing, including expedition-weight underwear. Some of the finest cold weather clothing— and the priciest—is made by Northern Outfitters. The company makes not only great cold weather togs, but also a superb synthetic sleeping bag system good to temperatures up to –60°F.

Clothing, though, will be the least of your worries. First should be obtaining a polar bear tag, and next should be coming up with the money to pay for your hunt. Polar bear tags are hard to come by. Jerome Knap, of Canada North Outfitting, had thirty-five tags available for 2002, but admitted that "only about twenty are legal for areas where bears are importable back into the United States.

"Some of these tags are for areas where bears aren't in any trouble," Knap said. "Not allowing them to be imported into the United States is a politically based decision rather than one based on sound bear management principles. But tags for most non-importable areas are properly designated as such. In the past the Fox Basin area, for example, was overharvested."

Most of Canada North Outfitting's hunts are conducted from Arctic island communities such as Arctic Bay, Broughton Island, Clyde River, Igloolik, and other Nunavut villages with a high harvest quota of polar bears.

Jerome's polar bear tags are sold out until after 2005, even at a cost of almost $23,000US for a single hunter. This cost usually includes the services of an experienced, licensed, Inuit (Eskimo) polar bear guide; a dog team available for the hunt's duration, if needed; the loan of suitable Arctic clothing; all food; field preparation of the trophy; and ground transportation by snowmobile from the nearest commercial airport to the hunting area or outpost camp and return. Nonhunting companions, like a spouse or friend, must also pay. If one or more nonhunters accompany the hunter, they are transported on a sled pulled by a snowmobile unless other arrangements are made.

The hunt's cost excludes travel from the hunter's home to the commercial airport nearest the Arctic community where the hunt is scheduled to take place; any air charters required; the license fee; export permit fees; personal effects; guns and ammo; excesss baggage charges; gratuities; packing and shipping of the trophy; taxidermy

Many polar bear hunts are conducted from Arctic island communities such as Arctic Bay, Broughton Island, and Clyde River. (Courtesy: Canada North Outfitting)

fees; cancellation insurance; and the Canadian goods and services tax of seven percent.

A polar bear hunter travels by dogsled over frozen floes of ice, listening to the wind, the hiss of snow, and the clatter of the ice. The icy formations beneath the sled's runners heave and creak and moan as the sled slides farther and farther from the

Temperatures in a polar bear camp can sometimes dip below minus 40-degrees F. (Courtesy: Canada North Outfitting)

guide's village. The actual hunt may take place as much as a hundred miles from the village. Meanwhile, the hunter and guide spend little time communicating, since neither speaks the other's language. The guide and dogs do their work while the hunter tries to stay warm in borrowed caribou-hide clothing.

When a bear track large enough to be worthwhile is finally cut, the guide and sled follow the trail. The hunt continues like this until the guide spots the bear ahead of him. In time-honored Inuit fashion, the guide then releases the sled dogs to chase after and harry the bear. The bear is often more perturbed about the dogs than it should be, and sometimes it makes a desperate bid to escape, leaving the dogs milling about in confusion, not sure whether to follow its trail or wait for the hunter.

If a bear is wise to the ways of the dogs, it will sometimes attempt to lose its pursuers in a nearby rugged area of icy bluffs and pressure ridges. A bear can easily disappear among such formations, and only relentless pursuit will reveal him to the hunters.

The bear is usually not far away, but sometimes a shot can be challenging because the sled dogs are hard to call off, especially when the bear continues to charge at them. Hunters must carefully choose their shots—the Inuit guides are not exacty thrilled at the prospect of losing one of their dogs.

Eskimo sled dogs harry the polar bear until the hunter can get into position to take his or her shot. (Courtesy: Canada North Outfitting)

POLAR BEAR QUOTAS

Before CITES (Convention on International Trade in Endangered Species of Wild Fauna and Flora) stepped in, and before the passage in 1972 of the Maritime Mammal Protection Act (MMPA), guides flew over the polar ice cap in search of roaming polar bears. If they located one, they landed a small plane on skis as close to the animal as possible. Hunters sometimes walked only a short distance before shooting a bear. Such so-called "hunting" practices were rightfully perceived as being anything but fair chase.

After the MMPA's passage, each Inuit or Inukliat village was awarded a certain number of permits that could be used to hunt the white bears in the traditional manner. The Inuit guide would cut a track and use a dogsled to get as close as possible to the bear. When he was very close, he released his sled dogs to bring the bear to bay. While the bear was occupied with the dogs, the hunter rushed in close to the bear and plunged his lance or harpoon through the bear's ribcage. Today's hunt differs mainly in the weapons used. Inuits guide hunters who use firearms, including muzzle-loaders, and bows. The Inuit people also continue to hunt polar bears themselves for native crafts and tribal ceremonies.

Polar bear hunting very often becomes a test of endurance. Some hunters nearly lose their minds from sheer boredom unrelieved even by anything resembling a normal meal. Others tire quickly of the bitter cold. Unexpected storms can turn into whiteouts, when all hunters and their guides can do is crawl inside a cold tent to wait for better conditions. And frostbite is a real possibility. More than one polar bear hunter has traveled north with intact fingers and toes only to return missing several digits.

Almost every hunter with a tag will take a polar bear. "Most of our hunts won't end until the bear is bagged," Jerome said. "Hunters should not book a polar bear hunt if they must be home immediately after the hunt. Not only might weather be a factor in whether they will be able to leave, but also, if a bear has not been taken, the Inuit almost insist on guiding hunters until they take a bear. This could tack several days onto the hunt, so keep a flexible schedule."

CITES has made the

Polar bear hunting often becomes a test of endurance. (Courtesy: Canada North Outfitting)

Polar bears are a valuable Eskimo commodity. (Courtesy: Canada North Outfitting)

importation of polar bear trophies interesting, to say the least, but Jerome Knap said he rarely has problems with the U.S. Fish and Wildlife Service. "Hunters who tells officials off are going to get in trouble," Jerome said. "My theory is that you'll attract more bees with honey than with vinegar. Be nice to the agents. Be respectful. Most of the time they will work with you to get your bear back into the United States."

Jerome counseled hunters thinking of hunting the great white bears with either a muzzle-loader or a bow to go no smaller than a .50 caliber black-powder gun. "Nunavut law requires archers to use nothing less than a bow with forty-five-pound draw weight," he said. "We tell them to bring a sixty-five-pound bow."

Surprisingly, Jerome has had few problems with hunters being injured by bears. "One of our worst experiences was when a bowhunter arrived at the airport but his quiver didn't," Jerome said. "He had only three arrows with him and no chance of replacing them in camp. He went hunting anyway, but his bear had to be finished by a backup shooter. To the guy's great credit, he didn't complain. He never said the bear was killed with a bow, either.

"When the village council is awarded its annual quota of polar bear tags, it immediately sets aside a certain number of tags for sport hunters," Jerome explained. "They then contract with me, and once I know how many tags are available I start booking hunters or contacting those who aren't yet sure they will be able to get a tag that year.

"The season generally runs from October 1 to May 31 or until the polar bear quota has been reached. This quota varies from village to village, or from one bear management zone to another.

"Some people don't like the fact that visitors can travel to the Arctic and kill polar bears," Jerome continued. "But polar bears are a valuable Inuit commodity, whether the bears are being hunted, photographed, or just observed."

BRUCE PELLETIER'S HUNT

Bruce Pelletier, who owns and operates Gentle Ben's Lodge in Rockwood, Maine, is a dyed-in-the-wool bear hunter who had initiative enough to find his own way to hunt polar bears. In 2000, Bruce bypassed booking agents and outfitters to contract on his own with an Eskimo named Charlie Reuben. "I flew into Inuvik in the Northwest Territories," Bruce said. "I bought my permits directly from the Eskimos. Ordinary people can't do this, but I have a friend who arranged everything for me, so I was able to get away with it. I saved $5,000 over the ordinary cost of a polar bear hunt like this."

And what a hunt Bruce had. He piled into his dogsled with his Eskimo guide while another Eskimo followed on a snow machine. "I really didn't know what to expect," Bruce said. "I saw seven polar bears in an eight-hour hunt. I first saw a mother with two cubs that we stayed clear of. We then spotted a seven-foot bear and then one that would have measured about eight feet. My guides urged me to shoot one or the other of these two bears, but I wanted something bigger. I passed them both up."

"We continued over the snow," Bruce continued. "It was forty degrees below zero when I went in mid-March. I was all bundled up when Charlie spotted a huge track in the snow that covered the ice. That track measured fourteen inches across. I knew it was just a huge bear. Charlie could speak excellent English. He told me you don't see tracks like that very often."

"We continued for another forty-five minutes before I saw the bear," Bruce said. "When I first spotted him, he was standing erect on his hind legs staring at us. He was still two hundred yards away, so I wasn't able to tell how big he was. After all, the bear's coat is white and everything around him is white, so it's somewhat difficult to know what you're looking at. I knew the track was huge, though, so I knew it had to be a big bear."

Bruce prepared for the shot as the bear dropped back down on all fours. He settled the cross-hairs on the big bear's shoulder and squeezed the trigger. The .300 Win Mag roared and bucked, and a 200-grain Nosler Partition bullet slammed into the bear. "That first shot would have done him in," Bruce said. "But my guides kept telling me to shoot, so I did, twice more." Bruce's second shot again hit the bear in the shoulder, while the third entered the big bruin's heart.

When the triumphant hunters returned to the village, an old woman who had been fleshing polar bears for her entire life told Bruce it was the largest bear she had ever seen.

Was it ever! The hide squared eleven feet. And the skull, unbelievably, may be the new world record. When Bruce brought the hide and skull to his taxidermist, he didn't pay much attention to what it might score. Only later, during the interview for this book, did he mention that his taxidermist had said the big bear's skull green-scored 30 using the Boone and Crockett system. The current record was taken in 1962 and scored 29 15/16. Even if Bruce's magnificent bear scores less than that, it will still rank in the top five polar bears ever taken, an incredible feat in itself! The second-ranking polar bear, from 1965, measured 29 1/16, and two bears, from 1958 and 1967, tied for third place with scores of 28 12/16. Bruce's bear could very easily be the new world record as well as the only polar bear out of Boone and Crockett's top 75 to have been taken more recently than 1967.

REGULATIONS

Any hunter wishing to export a polar bear must abide by the treaty regulations as they appear in Annex II of CITES, which mainly stipulate that a polar bear hunt must be done by dogsled. Hunters can obtain CITES permits in various villages, including Iqaluit (formerly Frobisher Bay), Arviiat (formerly Eskimo Point), Coppermine, and Yellowknife. Canada North Outfitting can also get them in Ottawa.

Gianbattista Lecco took this magnificent bear with Canada North Outfitting in 2000. (Courtesy: Canada North Outfitting)

Meanwhile, hunters who wrestle with their friends and neighbors about the legitimacy of their hunting an animal still considered "endangered" can commiserate with Noah Kadlak, an experienced native polar bear hunter who asked for permission to stage a true traditional Inuit hunt, which was to have been filmed by a Canadian production company.

Nunavut's minister of sustainable development turned Kadlak down, saying, "It's a new world now, a modern world, and we have to look at other issues."

A court ruled that the minister's concern was no reason to deny Kadlak the hunting permit. After consulting with eleven Inuit elders, the minister confirmed his decision, citing safety, although Kadlak would have been backed up by a team of armed hunters.

Officials in Nunavut really feared that the hunt would harm the fledgling territory's public image.

Despite the fears of Nunavut officials, many hunters from every corner of the globe continue to believe that hunting the white bear of the North in its own icy environment is one of the world's most fantastic adventures.

BIG BORES FOR DANGEROUS BEARS

It makes no difference how big or how dangerous the game is, the most important factor in being able to bring an animal down quickly and humanely is the accuracy of your firearm. This is true whether you're packing a .270 Win or a .460 Weatherby. Both will easily kill a bear, even one that tips the scales at fifteen hundred pounds or more, *if* the animal is hit properly. Both guns will also easily wound a bear, too. And that's a situation you—and your guide—want to avoid at all costs.

So how much gun is too much gun? Strictly speaking, that depends on the hunter. I know petite women who have small skeletal structures and weigh less than a hundred pounds who shoot the largest bores they can find. Coni Brooks (American Fork, Utah), Phyllis Tucker (Muncie, Indiana), and Gloria Erickson (Holdredge, Nebraska) all fit into this category. Small but mighty. Phyllis Tucker, though, is one big-bore rifle buff who might not have chosen to shoot magnums had she known any better when she started hunting.

"I learned to shoot with a .300 Weatherby," she said. "I had to get used to it, because I thought all guns kicked like that."

Phyllis was determined to go hunting. Her husband was equally determined that she not go hunting. She had no help from anyone, so she simply went into a gun store and bought the first gun that caught her eye. She became a phenomenal shot and a fantastic hunter, and so far has taken many species of bears, including some huge black bears, an Alaskan brown bear, and a grizzly. Obviously, she is able to handle quite well the recoil a big bore can deliver.

When you're bear hunting, accuracy should outweigh all other considerations. If you can't shoot accurately, it really doesn't

"I thought all guns kicked like that," said Phyllis Tucker, after shooting her first gun, a .300 Weatherby Mag. "I didn't know any better." (Courtesy: Larry Heathington)

matter much what caliber rifle you choose, especially when your quarry is the black bear. Common sense must prevail when going after a brownie or grizzly, however, particularly if you're thinking of heading out with a .243 Win. The point is, poor shooting is poor shooting, and a gut shot is a gut shot, whether the animal was slammed with a .338 Win Mag or a .30/30.

To become adept at killing bears, you must first understand them. You have to realize right away that bears have a desire to live unlike that of any other animal. When a wounded bear's adrenaline is flowing, if it knows who or what is responsible for its pain, look out. It can take a lot to bring that bear down.

A NEAR DISASTER

My good friend Dalton Carr of Craig, Colorado, told me the following story, which is also found in his great book, *Tales of a Bear Hunter,* to illustrate the tenacity and toughness of a wounded and enraged bear. On this occasion Dalton, who once worked as a predator control officer for the Yakima Nation in Washington State, was fortunate enough to hunt with one of the greatest bear hunters of all time, C.E. Barnett. Barnett worked for the American Fish and Wildlife Service, the precursor of the U.S. Fish and Wildlife Service. C.E. Barnett killed well over twelve hundred bears, many of them grizzlies, during his long and industrious career. On this particular occasion, Dalton and C.E. were guiding another hunter to his first black bear. This third hunter, Harold, was packing a .300 Weatherby loaded with 220-grain Barnes bullets. As Dalton remarked, "It seemed like enough to do the trick."

"We should have known we were in trouble when Harold asked us at least five times before we reached our destination, "Tell me again, where should I hit him?" C.E. and I knew his confidence was failing fast, and we should have declined to take him any farther, but we said nothing.

The hunters approached the mountain to be hunted and traveled along an old road, listening for the sound of rocks rolling upslope that would reveal the presence of a bear digging for marmots. When they finally heard the telltale *clunk, clunk, clunk* of rolling talus, C.E. whispered, "There he be, let's go get him."

The hunters could see a huge black rump sticking out of the bank about 125 yards above them. C.E. was carrying a bear call that imitated the cries of a badly injured marmot. He planned to use the call as soon as the hunter said he was ready. When the bear turned around to look for the source of the sound and C.E. told him to shoot, the hunter was to put a bullet through the bear's shoulders.

"C.E. blew twice on the call," Dalton said. "Sure enough, the bear pulled its head out to look for the marmot."

"Shoot," whispered C.E.

"Now?" said the hunter.

"Shoot," said C.E., with more intensity.

"Now?" said the hunter.

The bear lost patience, stuck its head back in the hole, and continued digging. "That bear's not going to dig forever," C.E. said. "When I say, 'shoot,' you shoot." C.E. blew the call again. The bear pulled its head out of the hole and turned sideways. The opportunity was perfection itself.

"Shoot!" said C.E.

"Now?" said the hunter.

The bear returned to digging. "C.E., who was a very religious man whom I had never heard curse, now said, 'Dammit. That bear's going to get our scent or hear us any minute now. When he does, he'll be gone. When I blow this time, you shoot!'"

The scene repeated itself, with C.E. blowing the call, telling Harold to shoot, and Harold questioning C.E. Only this time, as the bear put its head back in the hole, Harold shot belatedly. "With a resounding thump, the 220-grain Barnes walloped the bear right square in the rump," Dalton said.

"Bears do not growl, they roar," he continued, "which is what this one did. The bear stood on the skyline, searching for the cause of its pain and discomfort."

"At that moment, the bear was mighty mad, and its eyes were focused on C.E., Harold, and me. With unbelievable speed, it launched itself into a charge down the slope, its jaws popping like a .22, and a six-foot-long string of saliva trailing from its mouth. Its ears lay back along its neck. Yep, this was a real charge! No bluff here!

"C.E.'s .300 Weatherby fired, and dust and hair flew from the bear's shoulder as a 180-grain Nosler smashed into bone. Its shoulder caved in, and it flipped over into two somersaults before continuing its charge.

"I now shot my .358-99 Savage," Dalton said. "The bear rolled, but rose again and continued its rush. Its saliva was now streaming red, but it was still roaring in between bawls of pain. I shot again and the bullet kicked up dust on the bear's chest.

"Now C.E. fired a second time. The bear tumbled three times, hit the bottom of the slope, regained its footing, and was now thirty-five yards away and coming straight at us. C.E.'s rifle boomed a third time.

"It was twenty yards away when I realized I had to adjust my aim," Dalton said. "I had been shooting just inside the shoulder socket. I now aimed an inch and a half farther to the left and touched off the last shot I would be capable of firing before the bear would be all over us. The shot was good. The bear slammed forward on its chest, its front legs trailing helplessly beside its body. It pushed itself through the shintangle with its hind legs till it was five yards from me. It was still full of fight. Dead, but not knowing it.

"I aimed my .44 Magnum and put a bullet into its brain, ending the most furious and determined charge I had ever witnessed.

"I heard C.E. say, 'I've gotta sit down!'

"When I almost tripped over Harold's .300 Weatherby lying on the shintangle,

The wise hunter always checks his or her rifle soon after arriving in bear camp. (Courtesy: Jim Zumbo)

I looked downslope and saw him, 150 yards away, running at full speed and leaping brush like a deer.

"'By golly,' C.E. said. 'That guy surely can jump.'"

That particular near-disaster occurred when two famous bear hunters, with detailed knowledge of bear anatomy, went hunting with the wrong man. Adding to their eventual predicament, they picked on possibly the worst bear in the world, at least on that particular morning.

Bears are tough. They are tenacious. To bring them down and do it quickly, hunters must have a good knowledge of bear anatomy, a good rangefinder or the ability to correctly judge distance, and the discipline to limit themselves to "money" shots—those they can make with certainty. Serious bear hunters must be proficient when shooting from sitting, kneeling, and standing positions. They should be able to quickly find a rest or be able to use a sling properly. They should shoot a gun of reasonable caliber that can accurately fire a bullet sturdy enough to bore through tough layers of muscle and bone. If they are careful when they shoot, they will succeed.

What caliber?

If you presently own a rifle chambered for the .270 Winchester, 7mm Mag, .280 Rem, .308 Winchester or .30-06 and can place all of your shots in an 8-inch circle out to two hundred yards or better from a sitting or kneeling position, you can be a successful Alaskan bear hunter.

Some hunters feel like they have an edge when armed with a larger caliber, like the various .300s, the .338, .375, or .416. More knockdown power is the reason they give, but that knockdown power affects the shooter, too, so keep that in mind.

Recoil damage to your body may not affect you for weeks or even months, but may show up years in the future. It is better to shoot a gun that doesn't bruise your shoulder, if possible, than one that does.

Most guides would rather have hunters who are confident with their rifles and can handle them quickly and accurately in dangerous situations than hunters who arrive with larger-caliber rifles that have hardly been fired. Alaskan guides and outfitters who have kept records of what clients have used through the years for brown bears and grizzlies— have some proof to support the contention that a hunter who is a good shot with a .270 or .30 caliber rifle will fare as well, or even better, than most hunters who pack more gun. Confidence in their firearms is the great equalizer among successful bear hunters.

That being said, it is an old axiom of the bear guide that to down a bear weighing up to six hundred pounds will require approximately two thousand foot-pounds of energy. To cleanly down a bear that weighs more than six hundred pounds, the rule of thumb is to increase the necessary foot-pounds to twenty-eight hundred. Using this formula, a distance of two hundred yards, and an eight-hundred-pound brown bear, a hunter shooting accurately with factory loaded ammunition could reasonably expect no problems killing the bear when using a .300 Weatherby Mag with 180-grain bullets, a .338 Win Mag with 225-grain bullets, a .340 Weatherby Mag with 200-, 210-, or 250-grain bullets, a .375 H&H Mag with .270- or 300-grain bullets, a .378 Weatherby Mag with 270- or 300-grain bullets, a .458 Win Mag with 510-grain bullets, or a .460 Weatherby Mag with 500-grain bullets.

An old axiom says a hunter needs 2000 ft. lbs. of energy to down bruins the size of these two, which were taken by Remington's Art Wheaton and Jim Zumbo. (Courtesy: Jim Zumbo)

The hottest new bear cartridges are the so-called 'short' or 'ultra' magnums like the Remington .338 Short Action Ultra-Mag, which was used by Jim Zumbo to harvest this big grizzly. Courtesy: Jim Zumbo)

More important than any other factor is asking your guide for bear hunting gun and ammunition recommendations. Then consider what you already own—as well as how well you can shoot it—before making your final decision.

MUZZLE BRAKES

Muzzle brakes reduce recoil, but they also increase muzzle blast. Muzzle blast not only is deafening, but the barrel flash is also enough to singe hair. Some guides refuse to let hunters use guns outfitted with muzzle brakes. Check with your outfitter or guide before your hunt rather than wait until you're already in camp, fondling a gun that you'll be asked to leave behind.

Short and Ultra Magnums

The hottest new bear cartridges to appear in many a year are the so-called "short" or ultra magnums. Included in this category are the .300 Winchester Short Magnum (.300 WSM) and Remington's .300 Short-Action Ultra-Mag (.300 SAUM), as well as Remington's .338 Short-Action Ultra-Mag. Spin-offs include Remington's 7mm SAUM and the .270 WSM. Winchester, of course, factory loads WSM cartridges, while Remington does the same for SAUMs. Federal provides a belated entry in the ammunition department with loadings for the .300 WSM, and more loadings are sure to come.

Short-action rifles are constructed with less steel in the receiver, bolt, and magazine. When ordnance engineers figured out that fattening up a cartridge case while also reducing its overall length provided downrange energy and trajectories quite similar to those of the longer magnums, hunters were the beneficiaries. They now could buy lighter-weight rifles, such as the Remington 700 Mountain Rifle or Browning's Micro Hunter, in one of these shorter-action magnums and yet sacrifice very little of the longer, heavier magnums' power or punch. At three hundred yards, when either a .300 WSM or a .300 Win Mag fires a 180-grain spitzer bullet, 2,150 foot-pounds of energy are produced three hundred yards downrange. Yes, the recoil energy is about twenty percent higher than when shooting a .30-06, but it still isn't bad at just 28.5 foot-pounds for the .300 WSM, as opposed to 23.1 for the .30-06 when each is shooting the same 280-grain spitzer.

The new .300 WSM is made by several popular gun manufacturers, including Browning, Ruger, Savage, and Winchester.

BOLT-ACTION RIFLES

Bolt-action rifles are considered more reliable and more accurate than other repeating-action rifles, such as the pump or lever action. More bolt-action hunting rifles are made than any other design, so it is easy to find such a rifle chambered for any of the popular bear hunting cartridges.

If you plan to hunt bears, you should plan to get intimately acquainted with your firearm as soon as you've made hunting plans. Knowing everything about the gun is imperative. You should be able to load it in the dark. There may be no time to spare for fumbling with a safety or inefficiently working a bolt that fails to chamber the next round. And of course, you must scrupulously maintain any firearm used for hunting bears—no one wants a bear gun to malfunction. Know the load you'll be shooting, too. Know trajectories out to and including three or four hundred yards. Memorize wind-drift tables. Consider taking along a bipod or shooting sticks, even though you might not use them.

When choosing a bear rifle, pay attention to the safety. It should neither flip on nor flip off easily, nor should it be extremely difficult to operate.

The bolt handle should feel good in your hand. Variations in the bolt angle and its positioning could mean the difference between feeling confident while afield or not.

The late Finn Aagaard, a well-known hunter of big and dangerous game, demanded that the guns he used for these animals be utilitarian first and foremost. Aagaard wanted a rifle equipped with sights that were functional at distances of fifteen feet to a hundred or more yards. It would have to be built tough, too, and be eminently reliable. He once wrote, "The choice of action for my ideal professional rifle is a good Mauser Model 98. No other repeating action can quite match the (German) turnbolt for reliability combined with accuracy."

Another well-regarded bolt action is Winchester's pre-1964 Model 70, which recently was reintroduced in post-1994 production models. Yet another desirable action is the Czech-made Brno ZKK 602 magnum-length action. All three actions rely on a non-rotating claw extractor for positive extraction and always-reliable controlled cartridge feeding. Their greatest selling point, however, is strength. These actions are more than up to the task of handling the heat and pressure produced by magnum loads fired from today's heaviest calibers.

Another point in the bolt action's favor is simply this: It is mechanically simple. When it rains or sleets or snows, and water leaks into your rifle's every crevice, crack and cranny, a bolt action is easy to take apart, clean, oil, and reassemble. Should you jam the barrel full of mud, or should a seed or other debris affect the firing mechanism, the problem is easily solved when you're using a bolt action.

Before you leave for your hunt, become thoroughly familiar with disassembling and reassembling your primary gun as well as your backup gun, if you take one. Bear hunting is no longer relatively inexpensive, and you might never again be in a financial position to afford another similar hunt. If your gun is inoperable, you may find yourself making a stalk on a dangerous beast as you clutch in your hand an unfamiliar rifle that you've never before fired.

STAINLESS OR NOT?

A serious bear hunter should strongly consider investing in a modern bolt-action rifle made of stainless steel and bedded in a synthetic stock. If you're bear hunting, rain, snow, fog, or sleet are almost a given. A bolt action is the most reliable choice when you know, going in, that weather conditions are likely to be poor, and stainless steel is the perfect choice for hunting bears because the alloy is resistant to rust. Browning's A-Bolt Stainless Stalker is my ideal all-weather bear rifle. Although stainless steel will eventually rust, it does so much more slowly than the ordinary carbon steels used in most rifles. So even if you're packing stainless, be sure to keep the gun wiped off, and properly oil it after each day in the field.

You might also choose to have a favorite gun's barrel and action Teflon-coated by a gunsmith qualified to do so. Never send your rifle or action to anyone who is just getting into this game, though. I did so once, and the smith dipped every metal part of the firearm, bolt face included, into the coating. The result was expensive repair bills, as well as a one-month spate of returns, arguments, and poor performance, since neither my firing pin nor my extractor worked any longer. The gunsmith did make good on his work, but I was not a happy camper.

THE NEW SYNTHETICS

Wood-stocked rifles simply cannot compete with synthetic-stocked models for bear hunting. Bad weather is a given when you're hunting bears. It is not uncommon to spend long days inside tents or lodges waiting for a storm or fog to lift. Weather doesn't always appear on schedule, either. Many are the hunters who set out to enjoy a beautiful day scoping the countryside for grizzlies or black bears but returned later that night soaked to the bones. Many, too, have left camp in shirtsleeves only to slog back that evening through a foot of newly fallen snow.

Sorry, but a wood-stocked rifle is not up to the task of bear hunting. A wet wooden gunstock will swell, and even a slight amount of swelling can make bullets spray all over a target, if they hit the target at all. Sure, your scope may return to zero when the stock dries out, but how long will that take?

No, synthetic stocks aren't as pretty as wood. And you're not as likely to get attached to a synthetic-stocked rifle, either. But such guns are today's workhorses of hunting. They won't fail you, no matter what the weather, barring some unforeseen catastrophe. Why take a chance?

DOUBLE RIFLES

In some circumstances it's just better to be safe than sorry. One such circumstance is when you need an immediate second shot, one packing some real oomph behind it. If that's the case, it's hard to beat a reliable big-bore double rifle. No other action can equal the double for reliability, especially if your life depends on getting off a second shot. Brown bears all have the potential to be extremely dangerous. Writer Robert Ruark was aware of this fact and always used the now-famous Westley Richards .470 double rifle when he hunted Alaska browns. Doubles may not be common among bear hunters, but packing one makes sense, especially when you're in thick brush, high grass, or close quarters.

What are the knocks against a double? Well, a double rifle is heavier than a bolt action, true. But that heaviness is not too noticeable because doubles are so well balanced. Typically the overall length of a double is between four and six inches shorter than that of repeating-action rifles. This is so because doubles lacks actions per se. When you're negotiating the alder thickets and tall grass common in coastal areas of Alaska or stalking quietly through dense British Columbia timber stands, nothing says "insurance" like a big-bore double. Perfect balance makes the double easy to raise, while its shorter overall length means fewer chances of getting hung up in the undergrowth. Bears are lightning fast and can be on you in an instant. A double in a hard-hitting caliber like a .416 Rigby would be ideal for anyone with deep pockets who's determined to take big bears in brushy country. A double rifle wouldn't be a bad choice for guides or outfitters, either, particularly when they find themselves cleaning up after a hunter's poorly made shot.

Following up bears that may be wounded and feeling murderous is never an enjoyable task. When you're outfitted with a quality double rifle, though, the chore becomes far less onerous because each barrel and firing mechanism operates independently of the other, making it extremely unlikely that both will fail at the same time.

The downsides to double rifles (besides weight) are five: expense, accuracy, recoil, jamming, and double discharge.

EXPENSE. Double rifles are very expensive due to the high degree of craftsmanship required at every step in the manufacturing process. Although you can expect to pay about fifteen times the cost of a basic bolt-action rifle, you'll have not only a slam-bam big bore but also a work of gunsmith art.

ACCURACY. If you plan to hunt grizzlies or brownies on the open tundra, you should choose a gun that will shoot well at reasonably long ranges—at least three hundred yards. Most double rifles are reasonably accurate to only about a hundred yards, though a few are accurate at longer distances. If your possible tactics include traipsing along well-worn bear paths near meandering salmon streams, where a giant boar or a sow with cubs could be on you in a heartbeat, a double could save your life. For quick shooting in close quarters when you need a lot of gun, you can hardly do better.

Accurate shooting, as Greg Jones of Kahles Optik knows, is the most important factor when hunting bears like this big bruin. (Courtesy: Jim Zumbo)

RECOIL. Yes, a double will produce it. If you aren't used to taking the punishment some doubles can mete out, you'd better stick with a smaller caliber that you can handle.

JAMMING. A double rifle is made to extremely close tolerances. Such precision machining may open the way for serious trouble from a vagrant bit of twig, a grain of sand, or a clod of dirt that could jam the gun's mechanisms.

DOUBLE DISCHARGE. Another possibility is that the barrels could discharge almost simultaneously. The second discharge is usually triggered by recoil from the first discharge.

If you dream of hunting big bears with a double, be sure to clue in your outfitter and guide about your plans well before you pack for your trip. They may have other ideas about what they think you should use for shooting bears, and theirs are the opinions that matter most.

BULLETS

How often have we heard the saying "Speed kills"? It's as true with your choice of bullets as with anything else. Speed kills. What does it mean? Well, even though a round-nose bullet can and does kill every bit as quickly as a spitzer or semi-spitzer bullet, if distance is involved you're better off choosing the spitzer. That's because a bullet with a pointed nose does not lose velocity as quickly as one with a round nose.

Consider the aerodynamically efficient design of a jet fighter. Do you see a severely rounded nose on this aircraft? Of course not. The jet is built to slide through the atmosphere with the least possible amount of friction. So it is with the pointed-nose bullet.

Speed kills. Added speed results in more retained energy, which translates into knockdown power. At two hundred yards, a pointed bullet may travel three to five hundred feet per second faster than a round-nose bullet. If the bullets have been fired accurately, both will kill a bear. A pointed bullet, though, will provide more punch, so the game may drop more quickly, lessening the chance that you or your guide will have to follow it. A pointed bullet also does not drop as quickly at extreme ranges as a round-nose bullet does. You should avoid taking extremely long shots, particularly at massively built bears such as the Alaska brown, grizzly, or Kodiak, but stuff sometimes happens. The pointed-nose bullet is better suited for longer-range shooting.

Of course, some rifles shoot round-nose bullets more accurately than they do pointed-noise bullets. Only through time spent on the range shooting a variety of loads and bullet designs will you be able to determine which is the most accurate for your rifle.

Partitioned bullets provide outstandingly quick expansion at the bullet's nose, but none below the solid crossbar farther back in the bullet for quick kills on dangerous game such as this polar bear downed by Rocky Hill. (Courtesy: Canada North Outfitting)

BULLET CONSTRUCTION

There's much more to a good bullet than just its shape. In the last several decades, bullet manufacturers have made a wide assortment of highly evolved bullets that not only retain speed, but are also constructed to maintain weight or designed to expand in a predetermined pattern. A bullet that sheds grains or weight as it enters an animal is losing more retained energy than it should before it achieves full penetration. And a bullet that fails to mushroom isn't providing the knockdown power that a hunter looks for. To recover a bullet that's shed its core can drive some hunters to a state resembling madness.

Ideally, a bullet must be able to hold together as it penetrates skin, muscle, and even bone to reach vital organs. No problem. Witness the bullet known as the "solid." It penetrates to perfection. In fact, a solid will often shoot right through critters, even moose or bears, leaving the animals dead on their feet but not aware of it. Animals shot with solids can sometimes travel long distances while leaving little blood trail. A solid is a poor choice for most big game and, in fact, its use is illegal almost everywhere.

The solid, even though it holds together phenomenally well, isn't the answer for big game hunters. The answer is a bullet that is yielding enough to expand as it pile-drives through the animal and expands in a manner that doesn't expend all of its energy in one fell swoop. That is, it should expand slowly enough to continue to penetrate while wreaking havoc along the way.

Modern bullets are typically constructed from a copper or copper alloy jacket overlaying a lead or lead alloy core. The tip or nose of the bullet usually reveals this internal core. Most hunting bullets are made so that their jackets are thinner near the bullet's nose and slightly thicker toward the bullet's base. Such construction controls the rate of expansion. The bullet opens quickly at its nose, but continues to travel as the rest of the mushroom develops. Speer Grand Slam and Remington Core-Lokt bullets are examples of this design.

Hunters were pleased with such bullets, yet as good as they were they sometimes failed. Then the partitioned bullet was created. Partitioned bullets are made with a tapered jacket that includes an internal structure that forms a rough "H" shape, with the crossbar an integral part of the jacket. Each end of the H is filled with lead, lead alloy, or tungsten alloy. The result is outstandingly quick expansion at the bullet's nose, but none below the solid crossbar farther back in the bullet. Expansion shocks and destroys a lot of tissue, but the core continues to drive the bullet deeply into bone, muscle, and vitals. Examples of this type of bullet are the Nosler Partition, the Swift A-Frame, and the Trophy Bonded Bear Claw.

With such phenomenal performance comes increased cost. To cover the increased developmental and engineering costs as well as the added manufacturing expense, bullet makers charge about twice as much per box of these shells as they do for ordinary cartridges.

SCOPES

What you've read countless times is the same advice you're going to read here: Buy the best optics you can afford. Schmidt and Bender, Swarovski, and Zeiss are all wonderful, true. But so is Leupold & Stevens, and for a fraction of the cost. Fogproof, waterproof, shockproof, and tough—all are required in a riflescope used for hunting bears, particularly big, dangerous bears. I am the all-time best test of a scope's toughness. Within two or three years my riflescopes are battered to a pulp, and yet my Leupold has never been off zero even once. I've shipped my rifles to Africa on airlines and shipped them back. They've been to Alaska in bush planes, without cases, but never missed a beat. Leupold makes tough, accurate optical equipment. What more is there to say?

The consensus among bear-hunting authorities for bear hunting through thick cover probably would be to buy a fixed-power scope in the 1.5X to 4X range, although a good variable that powers down to 1.5X or 2.5X would probably work just as well. If you'll be hunting barren ground griz or doing a lot of spot-and-stalk, then you might want to up that to a 2.5 to 8X variable. If you aren't sure what you're going to encounter, choose something in the 1.5 to 6X or 2.5 to 8X range—with sight-through gun mounts if you worry about your ability to take out a charging bruin. Realistically, though, just keep both eyes open when your scope is on its lowest power (1X to 2.5X) and you should be able to shoot well enough.

A crisp, clear sight picture is imperative in any scope to be used for bear hunting. So is light-gathering ability, since bears are often active early and late in the day. For the best results, look for fully multi-coated optics with coating formulations comprised of a combination of rare earth salts. Optics that are multi-coated alone will not be in the same ballpark, performance-wise, with any that are *fully* multi-coated.

A range finding reticle could pay big dividends, but not if a bear is coming at you fast and you're trying to remember what all those marks really mean.

Scope covers are a necessity. Look for a set that is easily removed, yet tough enough to withstand some abuse.

SIGHTS

No one advocates open sights for all circumstances—unless the person using them is your guide. Some shots may be taken at exceptionally close range, but unless you are an open-sight *savant,* and few of us are, you will probably be much better off using one riflescope combination for all eventualities. Familiarity—remember?

Professionals, who sometimes must track dangerous, wounded bears into thick cover, will sometimes equip their guns with iron sights. A good set of iron sights, properly installed and tested for accuracy, will survive Armageddon, and is weatherproof, too. Favorites include the open express sight or an aperture-peep sight. The

A good set of iron sights, properly installed and tested for accuracy, will survive Armageddon and Montana outfitter Billy Stockton agrees. (Courtesy: Jim Zumbo)

aperture sight is probably the fastest of all due to its large opening or "ghost ring."

As stated in another chapter, Larry Heathington, a bear hunting guide from Arizona, has had more than a few brushes with charging black bears. Larry simply uses his flip-up scope cover as a handy sight. "It's good for taking bears when they're twenty-five yards or less and closing fast," he said. "Take it to the range and practice with it first. You should be able to hit a paper plate every time at twenty-five yards. That's good enough to stop most charging bears."

Before taking anyone's word on this, test it yourself to see if it works for you.

MUZZLE-LOADERS

Most conscientious bear hunters use nothing smaller than .50 caliber muzzle-loaders. While some states permit hunters to shoot bears with muzzle-loaders of .40 caliber or .44 caliber or above, most dedicated black-powder bear hunters prefer to use a rifle of .50 caliber or more, and Alaska law bans muzzle-loaders of less than .54 caliber for bear hunting. When hunting bears with a muzzle-loader, accuracy is of paramount importance. So is knowing that someone you trust is backing you up if your first shot—and often your only shot—doesn't do its job.

Many black-powder hunters are leaning toward the use of premium bullets like those now being loaded in sabots. Traditionalists prefer bullets like Hornady's Great Plains (a hollow base, hollow point 425 grain bullet), the Black Belt from Big Bore Express, or something similar.

Modern Muzzleloader's Knight in-line disk rifles are ideal for bear hunters, since the ignition system is enclosed, and thus less likely to fail under damp conditions. Jim Shockey, an outfitter and guide from Vancouver Island, British Columbia, used a Knight disk rifle to take every North American species of bear on his way to achieving the coveted "29 Slam" with a muzzle-loader.

Not only are today's muzzle-loaders more reliable than older models, but they are far more accurate, too. Some are capable of shooting excellent groups at distances of more than two hundred yards.

Check with your outfitter before booking a muzzle-loader bear hunt to learn whether your planned hunting area has restrictions for those who hunt with these weapons and whether it's legal to use scopes on them. Outfitters or guides may also have their own requirements for muzzle-loaders.

Many hunters feel that they have better ignition under damp or wet conditions with black powder than with Pyrodex, but black powder is more difficult to transport. Check with your outfitter to see if you can have black powder shipped ahead of time if that is what you prefer to use.

Finally, always keep the guide to your left when shooting a traditional muzzle-loader so that exhaust gases won't burn him or her. This point is moot, though, when you're shooting an in-line design.

SHOTGUNS AND SHELLS

Not only do some guides and outfitters pack shotguns sawed off to a length that is still legal, but a few hunters also use shotguns to harvest bears where it is legal to do so.

Shotguns are usually reserved for the bait hunter or hound hunter who is almost guaranteed a close shot at a relatively motionless bear. Use a minimum 12-gauge shotgun loaded with slugs or sabot-slugs when hunting bears.

Some hunters will substitute 00 buckshot when it is legal. Outfitters and guides who must negotiate heavy brush while trekking through bear country have also been known to load up with 00 buck. A shortened double-barreled shotgun comes up easily, is usually well balanced, and can quickly convince an aggressive or

For muzzle-loaders, Thompson/Center Arm's new Omega .50 is an ideal choice fur hunting bears. It provides plenty of knock-down power and accuracy for this type of game.

belligerent bear that you mean business.

Hunters who must pack into grizzly country in Alaska or the lower forty-eight have also been known to carry larger handguns such as .454 Casulls, .44 Magnums, or other guns of blockbuster calibers. These are fine, well-engineered weapons, but be sure you are up to the task of shooting your pistol—and doing so quickly—if you're charged by a bear. Flinching has no place in bear camp if your goal is to protect your life or the lives of family members. Better to rely on your quick wits than to shoot a big-bore handgun and wound a bear that could very well kill you in return.

COLD WEATHER GUN CARE

Canada North's Jerome Knap, probably the continent's premier authority on Arctic bear hunting, shared this advice:

"When heading into areas where the cold may be extreme—and always when going after polar bears, your rifle must be winterized," he said. "Remove all oils from the bolt and trigger assemblies. Give extra care to the firing pin to be absolutely certain that all oil has been removed; otherwise the oil might congeal, which would keep the firing pin from striking the cartridge primer with enough force to ignite it. Then soak the bolt for five to ten minutes in a container of white gas (Primus stove fuel or naphtha), dipping the bolt in and out of the gas to be sure it is thoroughly clean. Hunters with semiautomatics, over-and-unders, double rifles, pumps, lever actions, or single shots must have their guns winterized by a gunsmith.

"Such rifles should be lubricated with graphite powder for use during periods of extreme cold.

"Hunting polar game is difficult enough if everything goes right. If your gun fails, though, your troubles have probably just begun."

BOWHUNTING BEARS

"Bears, poorly hit, can often be the toughest of all game animals to recover." That statement was made by my good friend M.R. James, editor emeritus and founder of Bowhunter Magazine. M.R. is a black bear bowhunting addict, having taken close to thirty black bears with his bow. "When a bowhunter fails to make a good shot, if the arrow takes out just one lung, or if it's an otherwise marginal shot, it can sometimes seem as though a bear can go forever.

"Bowhunters who think calling bears sounds exciting are right, of course," M.R. continued. "But they must remember that attracting a bear to a call means it will come in looking for you. That's not really an ideal situation. Calling bears isn't practical or wise for bowhunters."

M.R. was elusive when asked what he thought about the minimum draw weight of a bow that will be used to hunt bears. "Draw weight doesn't mean much today," he said. "It's the kinetic energy that matters. You can take a relatively light-pulling bow, say thirty or thirty-five pounds, but it's capable of delivering more than enough foot-pounds of energy to kill a bear dead. A hunter who shoots a thirty-pound compound bow from twelve yards away can kill a bear just as efficiently as if he were using a sixty-pound long-bow or recurve.

"Someone who has never hunted bears will have a difficult time imagining how much body fat these animals have," M.R. continued. "Ideally, you want a good exit wound to help you

Bears, poorly hit, can be the toughest of all game animals to recover. (Courtesy: Jim Zumbo)

Knowledgeable black bear hunters like Dave Dolbee probably would not use the same set-up as a grizzly or a brown better would choose, unless he was getting field practice for an upcoming hunt. (Courtesy: Dave Dolbee)

track the animal. If hit properly, a black bear will travel thirty to fifty yards before going down. The broadhead I prefer for bears would be a cut-on-contact point with a minimum of three blades, each of which should be sharp enough to shave with. Bears aren't nearly as thick-skinned as other animals, but they have such thick fur and so much fat that sufficient penetration can be difficult to achieve. I try never to take a shot unless I'm virtually assured that it will go through both lungs. A bear has the inner resolve to go forever. Even if you succeed in making a lethal shot, there is often so little blood that recovery can be very difficult."

M.R. is sold on two broadhead brands. "I'm pretty fond of Bruce Barrie's Titanium 125, which has a three-point replaceable blade head. Bruce's Rocky Mountain Archery sells a number of good broadheads. I also am sold on the stainless steel Phantom 125, the rights of which were recently purchased by Muzzy Archery. The Phantom is a cut-on-contact four-blade that weighs 110 grains without the bleeder and 125 grains with the bleeder. This bleeder blade is very solid. It's not flexible the way the bleeders were in the old Bear heads, which makes this a real improvement over the previous version."

Anyone who chooses to hunt the most dangerous game with a bow would be remiss to not investigate the most effective setup to use. The black bear hunter would not use the same setup a grizzly or brown bear hunter would choose. Likewise, other criteria would govern the choice of equipment to be used for hunting polar bears.

The territory of Nunavut requires archers to use nothing less than a bow with a forty-five-pound draw weight. Both polar bears and barren ground grizzlies inhabit Nunavut, and the minimum forty-five-pound draw weight is somewhat surprising since both of these subspecies can be difficult to bring down. Outfitters have a different take on this regulation. "We tell our hunters to be able to draw a minimum of sixty-five pounds," said Jerome Knap of Canada North Outfitters.

Archers must be well versed in the wildlife laws of the state or province in which they plan to hunt bears, which will make moot any recommendations provided here. To give an example of the detail into which some wildlife agencies will go when mandating what bowhunters may or may not use, here are Alaska's 2002 Bowhunting Regulations. Remember that every state or province may require something different:

REGULATIONS SPECIFIC TO BOWHUNTING IN ALASKA
- Archery equipment can be used during any general open season. Special bowhunter certification is not required for these hunts.
- Bowhunter certification is required for any *big game* hunt restricted to "bow and arrow only" or "certified bowhunters only."
- Alaska recognizes bowhunter certification cards from any state-authorized

program or the NBEF/IBEP card.

- Nonresidents applying for archery-only drawing permit hunts must enclose a photocopy of both sides of their NBEF/IBEP card with their application.
- Alaska's bowhunter certification course requires passing a shooting skills course. Hunters with certification from another state or the NBEF/IBEP card do not have to pass Alaska's shooting skills test.
- Crossbows and other weapons are excluded from archery-only hunts.

License Requirement

You must be in possession of a resident or nonresident hunting license and appropriate harvest ticket, permit, and metal locking tag. *No special archery license or stamp is required.*

Equipment Restrictions in Archery-Only Hunts or Areas

For all game, you may:
- NOT hunt with a crossbow;
- NOT hunt with a bow designed to shoot more than one arrow at a time;
- NOT hunt with expanding gas arrows;
- NOT hunt using chemicals or poisons or substances that temporarily incapacitate wildlife.

For all BIG game, you may:
- NOT hunt with a longbow, recurve bow, or compound bow unless the bow is at least:
- forty pounds peak draw weight when hunting black-tailed deer, wolf, wolverine, black bear, Dall sheep, and caribou;
- fifty pounds peak draw weight when hunting mountain goat, moose, elk, brown/grizzly bear, musk ox, and bison;
- only use arrows tipped with a broadhead that are at least twenty inches in overall length and three hundred grains in total weight;
- only use a broadhead that is:
- a fixed, replaceable or mechanical/retractable-blade-type broadhead when taking black-tailed deer, wolves, wolverines, black bears, Dall sheep and caribou;
- a fixed or replaceable-blade-type broadhead—not barbed—for the taking of mountain goats, moose, elk, brown/grizzly bears, musk ox and bison;
- NOT use electronic devices or lights attached to the bow, arrow, or arrowhead with the exception of a nonilluminating camera;
- NOT use scopes or other devices attached to the bow or arrow for optical enhancement;
- NOT use any mechanical device that anchors a nocked arrow at full or partial draw unaided by the hunter.

Alaska requires that an archer use a bow with at least forty pounds peak draw weight for black bear. (Courtesy: M. R. James)

BOWHUNTER EDUCATION REQUIREMENTS

- You may NOT hunt with longbow, recurve bow, or compound bow in any hunt or area restricting the taking of big game to archery-only unless you have first successfully completed a department-approved bowhunting education course (IBEP or equivalent).
- You may NOT apply for drawing permit hunts restricting the taking of big game to archery-only unless you have first successfully completed a department-approved bowhunting education course (IBEP or equivalent).
- Bowhunters wishing to hunt black bears over bait are required to complete an IBEP course if hunting in Game Management Units 7 and 14–16, and a department-approved bear-baiting course if registering in Game Management Units 7, 14A, 14B, 15, 16A, and 20B.
- The department currently offers the International Bowhunter Education Program (IBEP) course through volunteer instructors. The course includes a shooting proficiency test. Names of instructors and course dates are available at regional Fish and Game offices.

BOWHUNTING DEFINITIONS

BOW. A longbow, recurve bow, or compound bow; that is, a device for launching an arrow that derives its propulsive energy solely from the bending and recovery of two limbs. The device must be hand-held and hand-drawn by a single and direct pulling action of the bowstring by the shooter with the shooter's fingers or a hand-held or wrist-attached release aid. The energy used to propel the arrow may not be derived from hydraulic, pneumatic, explosive, or mechanical devices, but may be derived from the mechanical advantage provided by wheels or cams so long as the available energy is stored in the bent limbs of the bow. No portion of the bow's riser (handle) or an attachment to the bow's riser may contact, support, or guide the arrow from a point rearward of the bowstring when strung and at rest. "Bow" does not include a crossbow or any device that has a gun-type stock or incorporates any mechanism that holds the bowstring at partial or full draw without the shooter's muscle power.

BROADHEAD. An arrowhead with two or more sharp cutting edges having a minimum cutting diameter of not less than seven-eighths inch (7/8").

BOW PEAK DRAW WEIGHT. The peak poundage at which the bow is drawn through or held at full draw by the shooter at the shooter's draw length.

MECHANICAL OR RETRACTABLE BROADHEAD. A broadhead with cutting edges that are retracted during flight and open upon impact to a minimum cutting diameter of not less than seven-eighths inch (7/8") that does not lock open after impact to create fixed barbs.

BARBED. Refers to an arrowhead with any fixed portion of the rear edge of the arrowhead forming an angle less than ninety degrees with the shaft when measured from the nock end of the arrow.

MAKING THE SHOT

Bear hunters are always aware that at any moment, they could become the hunted. Bears not only are intelligent, but when wounded they may also become cunning. Add to that vindictive, and you can begin to understand why it is in the bear hunter's best interest to make every shot count.

All but the smallest bears can be termed "substantial" animals. Unlike the delicate skeletons of the various species of deer, a bear's bone structure is heavy. The bigger the bear, the heavier the bones. Even a small bear possesses a strength out of proportion to its size. A hundred-pound black bear could easily decapitate a person with a single swipe of its paw. It's difficult for people to imagine that a small, furry creature grubbing about under logs could turn into a crazed killer in the blink of an eye, but it has happened. Never sell any bear short. Like people, bear are individuals. While most of them want nothing so much as to be left alone, others may be spoiling for a fight even before a misplaced shot makes their lives miserable and their attitudes in sore need of serious adjustment.

A bear hunter knows that at any moment, he could become the hunted. Phil Mancuso with his trophy polar bear. (Courtesy: Canada North Outfitting)

Bears are sheer muscle, and their muscles are thick and dense. Late in the year, bears put on substantial fat that builds up just under their heavy, shaggy coats. Bowhunters should always remember that their broadheads must not only slice through a mat of coarse, thick hair, but also penetrate fat, muscle, and sometimes bone. Kinetic energy is lost with every succeeding layer of matter. Shooting a bear with a bow at distances greater than thirty or thirty-five yards is probably never a wise choice. Most bowhunters try never to shoot at a bear farther away than twenty yards. This is especially important when bowhunters are trying to take down a grizzly, Alaska brown, or polar bear.

Firearms hunters should aim at the bear's shoulder, not behind the shoulder as they have been taught to do when hunting deer or elk. If you can break a bear's shoulder with your first shot, you will anchor it to the spot. If the bear is unable to move, you can then kill it with your second shot.

Many hunters have killed bears by taking a head-on shot and aiming for the chest. This is an excellent choice if you can drill the animal through its heart, but it will also work if your bullet is constructed strongly enough to shatter bone that will then penetrate lungs and heart.

A spine or neck shot is tricky to execute, but is instantly fatal.

A shot at the rear end should probably not be attempted unless the bear is already seriously wounded, extremely close and you're packing a lot of gun, or your guide tells you to shoot.

Angle is always important, and a quartering-away shot can be very effective. If the bear does not know you are there, you can fire to take out its vitals. A bear that is oblivious to your presence as well as headed away from you will usually continue in the same direction after it is mortally wounded. It may also spin to bite at the place where the bullet or arrow entered, but its attention should be consumed by its annoyance, so it probably will not notice you and your guide. At least not if you're lucky.

Bowhunters should seek to slide their arrows in through both of the bear's lungs or its heart. Either shot should quickly kill the animal.

Should your first shot not drop the bear in its tracks, be extremely cautious when following its trail, especially if there is no significant blood trail. Even well-placed shots may not generate a trail that is apparent to those trying to follow the animal. Displaced hair and fat can clog entrance and exit holes, making trackers' jobs more difficult and nerve-wracking as they wonder whether at any minute the snarling visage of a wounded bear will rise up before them. Whether you're sure of your shot or not, if you did not see your bear drop, wait at least half an hour before following in its tracks. Even if you are positive that you killed it, do not, for an instant, drop your guard. More people have been killed or seriously injured by bears that they believed to be 'dead' than for any other reason.

Do-It-Yourself Hunts and Packing for a Bear Hunt

Some people would never consider hiring a guide to take them deer hunting. A lot of folks feel the same way about bear hunting. Why should they go to all that expense when they can do it themselves and do almost as well?

The reasons for hiring guides for hunting black bears are the same ones you'll hear for hiring guides for hunting white-tailed deer: Guides know where animals have been recently; they are good judges of size or quality; they might have hunting ground locked up or under contract; they may know ways to easily access remote tracts of public ground; they are set up to retrieve big animals like bears; and they could save a hunter's life in the unlikely event of a charge. And of course, in some areas it is illegal to freelance on a bear hunt.

The Do-It-Yourself Bear Hunt

Hunters with enough sense to completely check out ahead of time the legalities involved in hunting bears in their intended hunting areas will probably do okay. They will already know enough to get far off the beaten path for the best chance at a bear. They will also follow a checklist similar to this:

- Be sure you're up to the hunt physically. There is no such thing as being too fit. You must be able to hunt well and be able to take a good shot at an animal despite having exerted yourself a few moments previously. You must be prepared to follow your guide up mountains and down, through muskeg and creeks, and then help, if need be, to get the hide and meat back out. If you're hunting with your buddies, they won't be happy if you fail to do your share. Being physically fit is the key to a good bear hunting experience.
- Never go on a bear hunt by yourself.
- Before you leave, make plans for every eventuality. For example, who will shoot first if several of you are together when a bear is spotted? What will you do if it snows two feet while you're in the backcountry? At what point will you return? Who will be in charge of fetching and treating water? And so on.
- Determine ahead of time who will carry what. For example, only one hunter will have to carry the tent, so who will pack in the tent stakes and the tarp?

- Tell someone where you are going and when you plan to return. Set up a message drop so that your contact knows whether you made it out of the woods in one piece. If you don't leave a message, the contact should immediately contact the authorities where you were hunting. Leave the contact a list of emergency personnel to call in the area where you are hunting as well as their phone numbers. That way there will be no confusion or lost time if you fail to return at the appointed time.
- Pre-scout your bear hunting area by phone. Talk to game wardens, biologists, foresters, Bureau of Land Management (BLM) managers, and anyone else who might be able to tell you a place to hunt where bear densities are better than average.
- Make sure the firearm or archery equipment you're using matches the species you're hunting.
- Pack a compact gun-cleaning kit, including a rod with which to remove barrel obstructions.
- Pack a good quality bear spray (more on this later in the book). Consider buying a chest or waist holster so the spray is readily accessible in case of emergency.
- Pack a knife and sharpening stone.
- Never leave home without a compass, safety flares, signal mirror, space blanket, safety matches, and first-aid kit.
- Purchase up-to-date topographic and other maps and think about having them laminated to make them weatherproof.
- Bring along a compass even if you are taking a GPS. Leave the compass at home only if your GPS has a compass feature that works without a battery or signal. Remember that compasses become more unreliable the farther north you travel, and local anomalies and areas containing strong metallic ore bodies will cause incorrect compass readings. Topographic maps indicate areas where compasses will be inaccurate. When navigating through these areas it is wise to rely on direct map reading.
- Buy a good sleeping bag. Much bear hunting is done in areas of heavy or daily rainfall. Consider buying an expedition-weight (heavy) sleeping bag made of synthetic material that will dry out easily and will retain warmth even when wet.
- Carry a Thermaseat Therma-Pad to prevent the earth's chill from seeping through your sleeping bag and keeping you awake and uncomfortable all night long.
- Keep your backpack as light as possible. Consider buying an internal frame pack—it will improve your agility as you negotiate steep slopes or rockslide areas. Packs with highly flexible Kevlar frames are also good.

- Freeze-dried food is a necessity for saving weight, but if you can afford some extra poundage, take along some "normal" food to use as rewards. Candy bars, sausage, and cheese are all good. Be sure to store all food according to bear authorities' recommendations.

- Buy good optics and use them. Do not scrimp on your firearm, bow, optical equipment, rainsuit, or sleeping bag. Be sure you take binoculars that are a minimum of 8X40 or 10X40. Only fully multi-coated optics will really reach out there during the dimmer hours when bears are often active. Optics must be

Remington's Linda Powell and B.C. bear outfitter Darrel Collins buy good optics, and then use them. (Courtesy: Jim Zumbo)

fogproof, waterproof, and shockproof. Bear hunting can be brutal on gear and equipment. It's better buy the best and cry once than to cry every time you go hunting.

- Bring water treatment equipment or supplies to treat water you don't carry in with you.

- Try to wear as much polypropylene clothing as possible. Not only will it shed water, when soaked it dries much more quickly than other fabrics.

- Take along a good quality Gore-Tex rainsuit. It can be used in snow or high wind as an extra layer. On most backpack hunts, this set of Gore-Tex may be the only extra clothing you'll be allowed to take with you. If space and weight allow for it, consider packing a lightweight plastic rain poncho, too. It's better to be safe than sorry.

- Carry bungees or lashing straps for packing bear quarters or hide out of the backcountry.

- Buy a good pair of sturdy, waterproof boots with plenty of ankle support and heavy-duty soles that won't shred on tough terrain. The sole popularly known as the "air-bob" provides outstanding traction under almost all conditions. The air pockets molded into each of these bobs provide air cushion as you walk, while the many flexible surfaces serve to adhere to earth, mud, rock, and snow, even in areas where terrain is steep.

A good cookset and stove are well worth the investment. (Courtesy: Coleman Company)

- If you are hunting coastal areas, invest in a good pair of ankle-fit all-rubber hip boots or chest waders.
- Wherever it is legal, outfit yourself in complete camo, including face mask and gloves.
- Invest in a good stove and a cookset. MSR's Whisper-lite stove makes a dandy that breaks down into small pieces for ease in packing.
- Most bear hunters need no more eating utensils than a plastic cup and plastic knife and fork. If you must cut something, use your pocket knife or hunting knife.
- Carry toilet tissue, enough antibiotics to treat everyone in your party if pneumonia strikes, required prescription drugs, indigestion aids, anti-diarrhetics, laxatives, aspirin, eye drops, and sinus tablets. You'll also need sunglasses and sunscreen with an SPF higher than 30.
- Be sure before you leave that you have your license, tag, and all other documentation required while you are in bear camp. Check before leaving to see if cell phones will work where you plan to be hunting and then pack accordingly. Another option that would provide some peace of mind to individuals who will be packing in as a group yet hunting on their own would be two-way radios all set to the same channel for communication purposes. If you take such devices, it would be a good idea to pack extra batteries, too.

PACKING FOR YOUR BLACK BEAR HUNT

Black bear hunting is generally done during months when weather can turn nasty in a minute. Here are some other items you should include in your 'to pack' list:

- Hunting license, tag, and other paperwork;
- Gore-Tex hiking boots with good lugs and excellent arch support system;
- Hip boots or chest waders;
- Hunter orange clothing, as required by law;
- Wide-brimmed hat;
- Ammunition, if you're gun hunting;
- Arrows, if you're bowhunting, plus a small bowhunter's repair kit;
- Gloves;
- Plenty of socks;
- Long underwear;
- Small day pack or fanny pack;
- Camera, film, and flash; a self-timer may come in handy;
- Tripod for spotting scope and camera;
- A thick paperback book with small print to relieve boredom during periods of snow, fog, and rain;
- Fluorescent surveyors' tape to mark where the bear was standing when you shot and where the carcass is when you go to fetch help;
- Duct tape (see next section);
- Insect repellant and mesh clothing that protects against insects (see next section);

Bear hunters should invest in good boots with excellent arch support systems and good lugs. (Courtesy: Georgia Boot)

INSECT PROTECTION

Be sure to pack as though you will be in the thick of swarms of merciless bugs. You'll need one hundred percent Deet repellant and a spray can of permethrin to treat clothing against ticks. The permethrin will also kill mosquitoes or flies landing on you, although their death will be slightly delayed.

Always pack mesh gloves and a head-net. Use duct tape to secure sleeves and pants legs so black flies can't get inside your clothing and bite you, and consider duct-taping your headnet around your neck. Investigate bug-repelling clothing. Bug-Tamer and Bug Taboo make good insect-proof clothing. Wearing a hat cuts down on pesky, buzzing bugs such as no-see-ums that are attracted to hair and mucous membranes in eyes, nose, and mouth.

YOUR POLAR BEAR OR BARREN GROUND GRIZZLY HUNT

Outfitter and booking agent Jerome Knap, of Canada North Outfitting, was kind enough to provide his personal list of what hunters should pack for an Arctic bear hunting expedition. When you're polar bear hunting, it is usually possible to arrange to rent cold weather outerwear and sleeping bags from your booking agent, hunting consultant, or outfitter prior to the beginning of your hunt. Here is Jerome's list:

- Quality binoculars;
- Knife;
- Sharpening stone;
- Wool or insulated leather gloves with which you can shoot;
- Long underwear of wool or polypropylene;
- Wool socks;
- Wool pants;
- Wool shirt;
- Heavy wool sweater or light down jacket (all of the above items are worn under the caribou skin clothing that will be rented or supplied);
- Down or fur hat with ear flaps;
- Down, wool, or silk face mask or balaclava;
- Boot blankets;
- Down wind pants and parka (for walking in villages);
- Felt insulated boots (for walking in villages);
- Down or thermal underwear to wear as pajamas;
- Sleeping bag rated to –35° or –40° F.;
- Sturdy duffle bags;
- Twelve-by-twelve-foot canvas and rope if you plan to take your bearskin home with you;
- Game bags
- Forty to sixty rounds of ammunition.

Fly-In Hunts and Boat Charters

Fly-In Bear Hunting

Anyone familiar with Alaska knows how treacherous much of the state's terrain is. Tundra, muskeg, forest, and mountain ranges soaring high into the sky provide formidable obstacles, so there are very few roads. In some places there are no roads for many hundreds of miles.

Nonresidents may hunt black bears in Alaska without guides. Hunts for other bear species require the services of a licensed guide. Do-it-yourself black bear hunters usually hire air charter services to fly them into hunting areas. Air charter operators are licensed by the state to charge for flying hunters and their game meat.

Every year a few nonresident hunters with pilot's licenses and airplane access decide to act as their own air charter service. This may be the most foolish choice these folks will ever make. During hunting season, Alaska's weather is bad as often as it is good. Strong winds buffet small planes about, heavy rains lash at the crafts and severely limit visibility, and sudden bursts of cold air can ice carburetors and make engines cough, sputter, and miss, if not worse. Pilots must contend with fog and blizzard conditions, each of which can make navigating through some of the mountain ranges particularly dicey if they're not sure where they're going or which landmarks to look for. I once flew in a bush plane that tried three times to fly through a narrow pass and all three times ended in loop-de-loops as sheer rock closed in on us from the front, left, and right. Each time the pilot executed this maneuver, we experienced several Gs of force, and soon I was screaming at him, "Land!" After he did—in a dry riverbed—my husband Bob and I spent a restless night after praying ourselves to sleep. We awoke to blue skies, took off again, and headed right back into a terrible storm. The pilot's next two attempts were similar to those of the preceding evening. When finally the clouds lifted so that we could see through the pass, I was so happy I would have kissed the pilot if I hadn't been strapped into one of the plane's two rear seats.

Actually, every time but once that I've flown in an air taxi or bush plane, I've had reason to fear for my life. The pilots were good, but the conditions became terrible—and quickly, too. Once our radio broke down when we were preparing to land at Fairbanks in a fogbank so thick we couldn't see the wings of our own small Cessna 185. Our pilot was quite worried, since Fairbanks handles jet airliners every day, and he instructed us to look out of the windows and let him know if we saw any big jets heading our way.

Yeah, right. By the time we saw one, we'd already be dead.

What I'm trying to say is, if you are not experienced at flying in Alaska, you should not consider using your own plane for hunting there. Harsh weather conditions are common there. A "good" landing strip may consist of a relatively flat, rocky riverbank or a small, shallow lake that will require a pilot with a floatplane rating (and, of course, a floatplane).

Hunters who want to reach back-country areas but don't want to pay a guide's exorbitant rates might want to consider booking a *drop-off hunt,* a

You can arrange to rent cold weather outerwear and sleeping bags beforehand from your outfitter when polar bear hunting. (Courtesy: Canada North Outfitting)

bare-bones-minimum expedition that costs considerably less than a fully guided or outfitted hunt. Your air charter covers all transportation for hunters, meat, and trophies. Most will also point out good hunting areas, and a few may even clear out a good campsite in an area where they have never before taken hunters. The hunters must provide tents, camp gear, personal gear, and food. Having an air charter involved, though, means that someone knows where you and your party are hunting. The air charter pilots are probably very familiar with the terrain and where game can be found. They are aware of how much hunting pressure each area receives during the season. All of these points are important, but the most important of all is knowing that someone will come back to either check up on your party or pick your party up, depending on what arrangements you've made and what fees you've agreed upon.

Air charter operators may charge flat or hourly rates for flight time, but these costs can be deceiving. Most hunters don't realize that operators have to charge them by the hour when traveling both to and from a hunting camp. In other words, the plane will make two round trips, and that is what the hunters will be charged for, even though on two legs of those trips the plane will be empty except for the pilot. So if you contract with a pilot to fly you in and then come back and get you after a hunt is over, and it takes two hours to fly you and your buddies to camp, you will be charged for eight hours: two in, two out, two back in to pick you up, and two back out.

Most air taxis are Cessna 184s and 185s. They can carry a pilot, two or three passengers, and some gear. If two or three hunters all take black bears, they may have to contract with the charter operator for additional trips to get the meat and hides out. These planes are not very big. They are not rated to fly with heavy loads. Air taxis are already subjected to the extremes of Alaskan weather, so there is no point in tempting fate by trying to fly when the plane is overloaded. Better to pay extra than to wind up like many Alaskan pilots and hunters do each year: crashed and burned.

A Beaver with floats can carry more gear, but it costs more, too. A Super-Cub is quite small. It can carry the pilot, one hunter and, at most, sixty pounds of gear.

FIGURING OUT HOW MUCH YOU CAN TAKE

If the plane you will be flying in has a payload capacity of twelve hundred pounds, you can figure out for yourself how much gear you can carry. If each person weighs two hundred pounds fully clothed, and two people will be hunting, the aircraft will be carrying six hundred pounds right off the bat (two hunters at two hundred pounds each plus the pilot at two hundred pounds equals six hundred pounds). So it seems that the two hunters in this scenario can each bring three hundred pounds of gear, far more than any hunter requires. What is important to remember about this equation is that you must have enough available capacity to haul out one bear if one hunter is successful. If each hunter brought fifteen pounds of gear and both are successful, the extra three or four hundred pounds of capacity will probably not be enough to cover the weight of two boned black bears and their green hides. So before booking with an air charter company, check to make sure that the cost of a meat haul is included in your price. Some include it, but others do not. Neither method is right or wrong. They are just different, but understanding what's covered up front can save you headaches—and money—later on. Whichever size plane you charter, pack your gear in soft-sided bags if possible. Pilots must sometimes cram gear into tight spots to get it to fit in their planes, and rigid containers or hard-sided bags aren't flexible and take up valuable space.

SPECIAL PACKAGES AND OPTIONS

Make sure to find out whether your air charter operator has any special package or flat-rate deals. Both are set up so that a hunter pays a single fee. Check ahead of time to see whether the package includes flying out the meat and hide. In flat-rate deals, remember that the operators win if game is nearby or if hunters are unsuccessful, because they won't have to fly as far to pick up game or won't have to pick it up at all. The hunters win when they take animals farther from camp than the operators expected or any time they are successful, particularly with large bears.

Another option included in some air charter packages is checking on a hunting party during the hunt. If this is part of the deal, and if someone is in camp, the pilot can be signaled to land and pick up game that may have been taken. If hunters know when the pilot will be returning, they can also be in camp waiting—particularly if they have been unsuccessful—and hitch a ride with their gear to a new hunting area.

Some hunters like having their air taxi fly them over a hunting area before they make camp. This is perfectly legal and is a good way to scout to see how much game is in the area. It is illegal to hunt on the same day you fly, however. The lone exception is if you have flown in a commercial airliner. Be sure to ask your air charter operator if such a scout from the air will cost you extra before you agree to it.

Hunters can get together by phone with bear biologists to pick out the area they would like to hunt. They can then request that pilots take them to that spot. Sometimes the pilots will and sometimes they won't. Perhaps they've seen bears somewhere else more recently. You have to decide whether you want to trust them or not.

They may know that there are a number of other hunting camps in the area you wanted to hunt. In that case they're doing you a favor by suggesting a different location. Discuss all the possibilities beforehand so the pilot knows what you are looking for and whether you are willing to consider alternate hunting locations.

Don't be disappointed, though, if the air charter takes you where you want to go but, upon landing, you discover other hunters nearby. There are many air charter companies in Alaska, and the one you've hired may have no idea who else is in the area until the pilot delivers you to your camp. And that doesn't even begin to take into consideration all the resident hunters who have access to their own aircraft.

If you absolutely do not want to hunt near others, let your air charter operator or pilot know this well ahead of time. They will probably be happy to accommodate you by taking you to a different location. But the decision to move could come back to haunt you, particularly if game is plentiful where all the camps are but scarce in an area where you'll be all alone in the wilderness.

Check references as thoroughly with an air charter operator as you would with a guide or outfitter. Your life depends on it, and so does the success of your hunting trip. Knowing what other hunters saw—and killed—during previous seasons is important. Don't forget to ask the tough questions.

Wanton waste is a very serious offense in Alaska, and the law regarding it is very clear: It is the hunter's legal responsibility to salvage all edible meat, skulls, and/or hides. Do not depend on the air charter operator to make sure you comply with the law. Learn how to properly field-dress a bear and get it ready to be flown to a meat locker. Air charter services almost always have access to meat lockers as a service for their clients. Conscientious hunters will arrange to have pilots periodically radio them to see if game is down or to provide pilots with a date on which they should return to pack out meat.

Many outfitters and guides conduct their bear hunts from boats like this one. (Courtesy: M.R. James)

WEATHER

When planning your hunt, keep the weather in mind. Besides making your hunting miserable, poor weather will often disrupt flying plans. Allow time on both ends of your schedule in case weather is too bad to get you in or out. If you absolutely, positively must be somewhere important the day after you're due to return from an Alaskan fly-in hunt, do not go on the hunt.

Never pressure pilots to fly if they are worried about the weather. This should be a no-brainer, but sadly, each year people make the fatal mistake of talking pilots into flying against their better judgment.

ALASKA BOAT-IN BEAR HUNTS

You can hire licensed boat operators in coastal areas or at various points along rivers to transport you to where bears may be found. Some services are geared toward fishing parties but let bear hunters ride along. When hunters sight a bear, the operator beaches the boat and the hunters get out to make the stalk. If they take a bear, the operator transports the meat and hide back to the takeout point.

Outfitters and guides also operate boats along the Alaskan coast. Hunters and guides watch the shoreline for bears feeding. When they spot one, the guide beaches, and the hunters get out to make the stalk. Hunting by boat is a very effective way to take a black bear.

HOW TO LOCATE LICENSED AIR CHARTER OR BOAT OPERATORS

When you request a list of Alaska's licensed hunting guides, you will be furnished automatically with a list of licensed transporters. Or you can access the list in PDF format on the Alaska Department of Fish and Game's Web site.

ALASKA'S PUBLIC-USE CABINS

Various state and federal agencies maintain primitive public-use cabins in some areas of Alaska. Most of them are accessible only by trail, boat, or floatplane, and you are not allowed to discharge firearms near most of them. Amenities are very few, with no inside plumbing. Users must supply their own food, cooking gear, bedding, water, fuel, and heater. Some cabins, but not all, have wood or oil stoves. Check before you leave on your trip to see which type you have reserved.

Agencies in charge of cabin reservations and rental are listed below. Most cabins are located in the southeastern part of the state. Go online to find out particulars of cabin rental from the agency in charge as well information regarding which, if any, nearby areas are open to bear hunting.

- Alaska State Parks
- U.S. Bureau of Land Management
- U.S. Fish and Wildlife Service

US FOREST SERVICE (BY LOCATION)

- Nancy Lake (Wasilla)
- Kachemak Bay (Homer)
- Caines Head (Seward)
- Chena River (Fairbanks)
- Shuyak (Kodiak)

Other remote cabins may be leased through the manager of the White Mountains National Recreation Area north of Fairbanks. In addition, two hundred cabins are available in the Tongass and Chugach National Forests.

Some cabins have a three-night maximum. Check with each agency to see what other restrictions apply. Prices range from twenty to fifty dollars per night, depending on how many people can be accommodated. Kerosene heaters, when available, add to the rental fee.

CHOOSING AN OUTFITTER OR GUIDE

You've chosen where you want to go and what kind of bears you want to hunt. You and your spouse or hunting buddies have agreed on just about everything, in fact. All that remains is choosing an outfitter or guide. Where do you start?

Start at the beginning by asking your hunting buddies these questions: Have you ever hunted in the state or province where we're headed? Do you know someone who has hunted there? Ask the same questions of members of your hunting club, if you belong to one. Ask the club's secretary to inquire in the club's next newsletter whether anyone has hunted with a guide or outfitter where you'd like to go.

Pay attention to hunting shows, outdoor travel conventions, and hunting symposiums. Outfitters often attend such events, where they set up booths, visit with potential clients, and hand out promotional materials. Talk to the outfitters or guides one on one. Ask them for references and ask to see photos of hunters. Don't be afraid to ask what animals they've taken and what year they were taken in. That's part of the investigative process. Ask what their success rate is. Ask what factors can affect hunting success in their areas. Ask about the best time to hunt the bear you'd like to take. The most important thing to obtain is a list of current references.

A number of suitable outfitters and guides should attend any major outdoor show. If you still feel like you might be missing out on something, read outdoor magazines. Look through the advertising in the back sections of most of them. Pay attention to ads for guides or outfitters who are qualified to take hunters into the state or province where you would like to hunt for the bear species you are interested in killing. Write or call these people and ask them to send you their promotional materials. Ask them to include a list of current references with the year they hunted and whether they were successful. Try to make certain that these individuals were hunting the same animal that you and your party want to hunt.

Once you've found some potential guides or outfitters, you have two tasks to perform: First, check to see that they are registered in the state or province where you will be hunting. Registered guides or outfitters are licensed to operate in a particular area. "Outlaw" or "rogue" outfitters have no such area license. After you've packed in, set up camp, and spotted a good bear is a mighty poor time to learn that your outfitter has no authority to be where you are. At best, you could be forced to move from the area. At worst, you could wind up with no guide or outfitter and little chance of booking another.

Cordova, Alaska's Sam Fejes guided Mike Fejes to this huge Alaska brown bear. (Courtesy: Mike Fejes)

Second, simply contact one or two references on every outfitter's or guide's list. If you are really zealous, check them all. Or divide up the task so each person in your group checks a portion of the list. The easiest way to do this is to telephone, but before you do, be sure you have written a list of questions to ask each hunter. Check with your spouse or hunting buddies (depending on whom you will be going with) to find out what they would like to ask. Ask each question in its turn, paying as much attention to what the hunters don't say as to what they do say. Some people are loath to speak badly of anyone, so pay attention to how the people you talk to construct sentences, choose words, and pause in their conversation, and you'll be able to tell if they were happy with the outfitter or seriously uncomfortable at lying to you about their experience. When checking references it is sometimes necessary to read between the lines.

Don't feel bad about putting people on the spot. They will either answer truthfully or not. After all, your hard-earned money is at stake here. Do not do as I did and spend a bundle on two ill-fated—and quite expensive—outfitted hunts before you finally figure out what to ask and why.

ISSUES TO CONSIDER WHEN CHOOSING A GUIDE OR OUTFITTER

Find out when you'll be expected to pay for the hunt. It is not uncommon for outfitters to request fifty percent of their fee when the hunt is booked, with the balance payable when the hunters arrive in camp—before any hunting is done. If outfitters agree to let unsuccessful hunters continue to hunt after a trip is over, the hunters are usually expected to pay up front for the extra days.

Be wary of outfitters or guides who guarantee you a kill. They might say their success rate is one hundred percent, but this is not the same as a guaranteed kill. Be sure to ask whether their success rate is always one hundred percent, year after year. A continuous one hundred percent success rate, while not unheard of, is somewhat unusual. Verify that figure with the outfitters' references.

Ask guides or outfitters what you will do if you tag out early. In some cases, other hunters may still be hunting while you are loafing around in camp. Outfitters who allow their hunters to fish or hunt upland game or have some other activity that successful hunters can engage in are way ahead of the pack.

Ask outfitters if there is a provision for allowing you to remain in camp until you bag your bear in case you have not done so by the end of your booked time. If you can remain in camp, find out what the daily rate is and when you must pay it.

Find out what outfitters require as a deposit and whether it is refundable under any circumstances. I have heard of hunters incapacitated by heart attacks or strokes a year or more before their hunts were scheduled to take place who were unable to obtain a refund. While I can understand outfitters refusing refunds a month or two or three before a hunt is to occur, or if it is a difficult tag to draw and the drawing is over, in some cases it is nit-picking to refuse to provide a refund if circumstances beyond the hunter's control somehow arise. Outfitters, of course, should have the option of applying the refund to a future hunt if that is satisfactory to the hunter.

Before you book your hunt, ask outfitters if the price includes:

- Transportation to and from an airport, and if so, which one;
- Air taxi charges (if hunting in Canada or Alaska);
- Any hotel or motel charges;
- All meals;
- Special food if you have dietary restrictions—and ask if this will be a problem;
- Field dressing the animal;
- Caping, either full body or head and shoulders;
- Transportation of the trophy and/or the hunter to the taxidermist;

Also find out whether your hunt will be a 1X1, 2X1, or 3X1 (one hunter per guide, two hunters per guide, etc.)

You should understand that if you kill your animal on the first day of the hunt, no matter how much you have paid your outfitter, there will be no refund. The outfitters have already made a significant cash expenditure whether you remain in camp or not. They have purchased food for the entire stay. They have hired guides for the week or two weeks that were booked, and so on. And outfitters are not responsible for bad weather. Never ask for a refund if your hunt is ruined because of too much snow, fog, or rain.

Finally, never ask outfitters to do anything illegal for you—this would be asking them to put their livelihood on the line for someone they don't even know.

TAKING FIREARMS INTO CANADA

Hunters who know the rules regarding the importation of firearms into Canada—and abide by them—should have no trouble getting across the border. The rules are fairly straightforward. Hunters must declare all firearms or bows when they enter Canada. At that point, Canada Customs officials issue temporary registration permits to nonresidents who enter the country with sporting firearms. When the hunters leave Canada after the hunt, they must surrender this permit to Canada Customs. No record is kept of the permit.

Hunters may not import pistols, revolvers, or automatic firearms, because Canada does not consider them sporting firearms.

TRANSPORTING FIREARMS

It is unlawful in Canada to transport a loaded firearm. This simply means that you may not carry in your vehicle or aircraft, whether it is moving or not, any gun with live ammunition in the breech, chamber, or magazine. You may not transport a

Any hunter who brings a bow into Canada must abide by the same stringent regulations that govern those importing firearms. (Courtesy: Canada North Outfitting)

loaded firearm in a boat, either, unless the boat is propelled by muscular power (rowed), or is at anchor and you are hunting. You may transport ammunition in a magazine as long as the magazine is not attached to the firearm. Hunters who bring bows into Canada must follow the same laws regarding their bows as the ones that regulate the transport of firearms.

Storing of Firearms
In Canada, if you leave a firearm in an unattended vehicle, it must be secured in a locked trunk or similar compartment. If the vehicle has no such compartment, the firearm must be stored out of sight inside the locked vehicle.

Returning to the United States with Firearms
Before leaving the United States, all U.S. citizens who travel to Canada or through Canada to hunt should register their firearms with the nearest U.S. Customs Office. This proves that you had the firearm before you left the country and did not buy it while you were away. Some citizens have been unable to prove that they left the United States with firearms in their possession and were forbidden to bring their "undocumented" firearms back into the States.

It is also a good idea to take cameras, binoculars, spotting scopes, and other high-dollar items along when you visit customs to register your firearms. Although it is less likely that ownership of these items will be questioned, it is always a possibility. If, when you reenter the United States, you cannot prove to the satisfaction of the customs official at the border that items were in your possession when you left the United States for Canada, they may be impounded.

Most major cities have U.S. Customs Offices, particularly those where an international airport is located. U.S. Customs also operates offices near many major border crossings, but be sure to make arrangements well before you plan to arrive to be certain such offices will be open. For peace of mind, it is better to register firearms with U.S. Customs well before you are scheduled to take your trip.

TROPHY BEARS

If you want to kill a bear large enough to qualify for either Boone and Crockett or Pope and Young record books, be sure to concentrate your hunting efforts in areas that are noted for producing bears with large skulls, but also choose areas that experience only a small amount of hunting pressure.

Most trophy bears must be between eight and twelve years old before their skulls are large enough to qualify for listing in Pope and Young's record book. A Boone and Crockett bear would almost certainly have to be even older, although younger individuals have, on occasion, qualified. Anyone determined to bag a trophy must first do his or her homework. Ask state and provincial wildlife biologists and game wardens if they know where bears in their areas live to the ripest old ages.

Trophy bears like this big black bruin usually are over eight years of age. (Courtesy: M. R. James)

Mary Parker's Toklat grizzly is a highly-coveted trophy animal due to its rare coloration. (Courtesy: Warren Parker)

Forage quality is also important when your goal is a trophy-class bear. Bears become larger where growing seasons are long and food is plentiful.

When sizing up bears, concentrate on their ears. All black bears old enough to be on their own will have ears of approximately the same size, and the same is true of grizzly bears. (But a black bear's ears will not be the same size as a grizzly bear's ears, nor will a large Alaska brown bear's ears be the same size as either a black bear's ears or a grizzly's ears.) So whenever you see a bear, look at the size of its ears in proportion to the size of its head. If a bear is big, its ears will appear small in proportion its head. If it's smaller, its ears will appear large. This holds true whether you are sizing up a black bear, a brown bear, or a grizzly.

"A younger bear will be lankier, too," said outdoor writer Jim Zumbo. "Smaller bears sometimes look gaunt or seem long-legged. A large bear's belly sometimes seems like it's about to brush the ground. If air is lacing beneath a bear's belly, shoot the bear—it's probably a pretty good animal.

"Hunters who put bait in fifty-five-gallon drums sometimes use those barrels to help size up a bear," Jim added. "If the bear's back is as tall as the drum, shoot it. It's probably a six-footer.

"If the bear's back is higher than the barrel's second ring, it will probably measure more than five feet, which is still a pretty good bear," Jim concluded.

On July 1, 1975, the Boone and Crockett world-record black bear skull was discovered along the edge of the Manti-La Sal National Forest near Ephraim, Utah. The immense skull was part of a carcass discovered decaying in the sun by Merrill Daniels and Alma Lund. The skull later scored 23 10/16 points, which is almost enough to qualify in the grizzly bear category.

Club-certified Boone and Crockett scorers measure bear skulls with calipers. The scorer adds the skull's greatest length (without the lower jaw and excluding malformations) to the greatest width (as measured between perpendiculars at right angles to the long axis) for a final score.

The current Boone and Crockett minimum scores for the various bear classifications are:

	Minimum Scores	All-Time Awards
Black bear	20	21
Grizzly bear	23	24
Alaska brown bear	26	28
Polar bear	27	27

The current Boone and Crockett Record Book reveals a three-way tie for the world's record grizzly. James G. Shelton, noted British Columbia bear authority and author, picked up a skull in 1970 in the province's Bella Coola Valley that scored 27 2/16. A year later another equally huge grizzly was taken in the same province along the Dean River by Roger J. Pentecost.

Then, in 1991, Theodore Kurdziel, Jr., bagged an animal as large as the preceding dual record-holders while hunting along the Inglutalik River near Koyuk Alaska. Kurdziel's bear charged him without any more provocation than merely glimpsing his presence, and the hunter fired at the giant bear's chest from a distance of about twenty yards.

The current world record Alaska brown bear scored 30 12/16 and was collected by a scientific expedition. The shot was made by Roy R. Lindsley, an employee of the U.S. Fish and Wildlife Service based in Kodiak. The bear was killed in May 1952, near Karluk Lake, Kodiak Island. Lindsey used a 180-grain bullet in a .30-06 rifle to kill the mighty animal. The skull is owned by the Los Angeles County Museum.

The largest polar bear recognized by the Boone and Crockett Club was taken by Shelby Longoria of Matamoros, Mexico, in the spring of 1963. Longoria hunted with outfitters out of Kotzebue, Alaska, to take his 29 15/16 trophy boar. Polar bears typically have longer, narrower skulls more suited to their swimming habits than those of the giant Alaska brown bears. Alaska no longer permits anyone other than native subsistence hunters to buy licenses for or kill polar bears.

The reward of a well-planned stalk. (Courtesy: Bob Beaulieu)

Boone and Crockett's scores are the gold standard to which all bears are compared. Qualifying scores for both the Pope and Young Club and Safari Club International are considerably lower. Pope and Young, of course, recognizes bowhunting achievements. Safari Club International (SCI) recognizes worldwide hunting accomplishments, including Amur bear, Siberian bear, Kamchatka brown bear, and mideastern (Eurasian) brown bear. SCI's minimum scores are lower than Boone and Crockett's, probably due to the club's practice of awarding various levels of hunting recognition based upon how many animals of a particular species, for instance bears, qualify for listing in their record book.

Preparing Your Bear for the Taxidermist

You've got your bear down. All that remains to be done is to take field photos and then do the hard work—the detail work—involved in preparing your bear for the taxidermist.

Line up your knife cuts with the areas on the bear's hide where hair lines separate to grow in different directions. (Courtesy: Jim Zumbo)

After the animal is field-dressed, someone must skin and cape it (see accompanying drawings).

DRAWING 1. Make cuts where shown to under-portions of the bear's body. Try to make the cuts between areas on the hide where hairlines or cowlicks separate and grow in different directions.

DRAWING 2. Now skin the bear to the back of its head. The lumps on each side are the ears. Grab these lumps and separate them from the skull by slicing them off as closely as possible to the skull.

DRAWING 3. Skin carefully to the animal's eyes and cheeks. Insert a finger from the fur side into the eye socket so you're aware of where you are cutting. Cut through the membranes around the eye—again as close to the skull as possible—and then cut through the cheek muscles and flesh to expose the teeth.

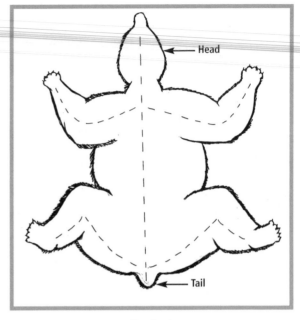

Drawing 1

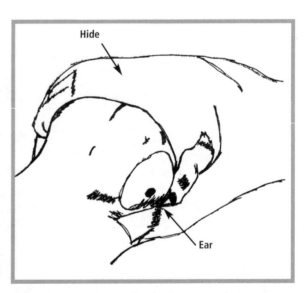

Drawing 2

DRAWING 4. Separate the lip tissue from the gums as close to the jaw bones as possible. Be sure to leave plenty of tissue from the bear's inner lips attached to the hide.

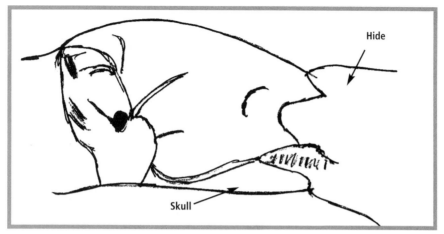

Drawing 3

DRAWING 5. Skin down the snout until you reach the nose cartilage. Cut through the nose cartilage as indicated in the drawing. You should now be able to separate the hide from the skull.

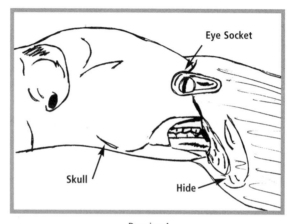

Drawing 4

HIDE AND CAPE CARE

The hide and cape must be transported immediately to a taxidermist or freezer—within one day in warmer weather and a maximum of two days in cold weather. Never transport or store raw hides in plastic or polyethylene garbage bags, because doing so could result in hair slippage–when moisture accumulates and hair begins to fall out. Instead store them in game bags and keep them in a cool, dry, shaded location.

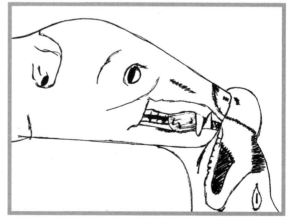

Drawing 5

An Eskimo guide will use a spiked sled to retrieve your polar bear trophy for skinning, caping, and fleshing. Evans Clyde poses with his Nunavut trophy. (Courtesy: Canada North Outfitting)

If you are unable to get the hide to a freezer or taxidermist immediately, you must remove as much fat, flesh, and other tissue from it as possible. Salt the bare skin heavily, especially around the animal's face and paws.

A medium-sized black bear hide will require between twenty and thirty pounds of salt, a grizzly between forty and fifty pounds, and an average brown bear between eighty and ninety pounds. Larger brown bears and polar bears may require more than a hundred pounds of salt to do the job properly.

To be sure of your field techniques, it would be a good idea to visit the taxidermist you plan to use and ask him or her to illustrate the proper way to prepare a bear hide and cape. If nothing else, the taxidermist may be able to demonstrate on a tanned hide that is being prepared to be mounted.

HUNTING LICENSES, TAGS, AND REGULATIONS

When it comes to buying bear hunting licenses and tags, never count on anything to remain the same from one season to the next, or from one state or province to the next. The very topic of bear hunting is controversial in some circles, although less so in states long traditions of the sport as well as solid bases of support from bear hunters. British Columbia, for instance, has a long and honorable bear hunting tradition, but recent inroads made by anti-bear-hunting factions in highly populated urban areas like Vancouver and Victoria have placed the entire bear hunting tradition and industry at risk. Add to this the ever-changing status of the landscape because of oil, gas, and timber exploration and exploitation. Each industry takes a toll on surrounding ecosystems—including the bears that inhabit them—and it is easy to understand why an area's permit issuance methods and quota systems may change from one year to another.

To illustrate the scope of what you must deal with today when planning your hunt, we will examine some of the restrictions, tags, permits, and licenses that you must be aware of. When you're planning a bear hunt, always call wildlife authorities or use a computer to access Web sites of state or provincial wildlife agencies with authority for the area you plan to hunt. Do this before doing anything else—even before selecting an outfitter or reserving vacation days at work. Things change, and they can change quickly. What is legal today—or affordable—may not be tomorrow. Bear biologists and up-to-date information posted on Web sites can keep you abreast of bear hunting trends before they happen.

In previous chapters you learned that some bear hunts are booked five years and more ahead of time. Although the bears that are the targets of these hunts— browns, grizzlies, and polar bears—are doing reasonably well in most parts of their ranges, license allocations do not always keep pace with increases in bear numbers. This may be a good thing, because the additional bears will breed to produce even more bears, and the net result should be a gradual increase numbers of tags available, barring some unforeseen bear calamity.

Once you have contacted a state or provincial game or wildlife agency, request a copy of their latest hunting regulations. These handy booklets are usually updated each year to reflect new or revised rules or laws. They provide a wealth of information to potential bear hunters concerning general seasons, license drawings, bag limits, and the legality of various hunting methods, especially the baiting of black bears or the running of that species with dogs. Some states and provinces—Alaska comes to mind—have a variety of permits available, but only some may be used by nonresidents. When you talk to the various agencies, ask them to add you to their mailing lists. Then you'll be sure to receive changes that are made in wildlife laws, application fees and instructions, and licensing, and you'll be one of the first to learn of new or special hunting opportunities.

Always refer to the regulations brochure for the legality of bear hunting methods such as baiting. Alberta, for example, requires that outfitters and hunters post warning signs on trees around the baited site. (Courtesy: M. R. James)

Some bear licenses and tags are sold over the counter to any hunter who wants one. When this is the case the hunt is called a *general season* hunt, meaning that it is open to an unlimited number of hunters. Do not be deluded into believing that a bear license is all that is ever needed to hunt bears legally. Some states also require hunters to purchase a *state hunting permit.* Alaska, for example, requires a *license,* a *harvest ticket* and a *game tag.* Noncompliance with any of these niggling and too often time-consuming paperwork requirements can usually be traced to hunters' failure or reluctance to do their homework.

Not all bear licenses are easy to obtain. Some, such as those for what are called *limited quota hunts, limited entry hunts,* or *drawing permit hunts,* may be quite difficult to obtain. Other than knowing that such hunts exist and that new ones may be established at any time, you must also keep attuned to various application requirements if you need one of these licenses where you plan to hunt. Some states and provinces use a system of bonus points which, once awarded, automatically provide hunters with a better chance of drawing in future license lotteries should they fail to draw in earlier rounds. Be aware, though, that some systems award bonus points only if the hunter agrees to let the wildlife agency in charge of licensing keep some predetermined fee, usually an application fee or permit registration fee. Sometimes this fee is only five or ten dollars, but at some agencies, it can represent a fairly considerable sum.

In some areas bear hunts may be conducted as *registration hunts*. Although this practice is not widespread, some states and provinces have started using such hunts to limit hunter access by allowing only a certain number of hunters into a particular area at the same time. Either the area to be hunted is too small to provide a quality experience for all the hunters who want to hunt there or only a limited number of animals is available for harvest. Requiring hunters to sign in prior to their hunts allows area game managers to keep track of hunter pressure and regulate it accordingly.

Another recent twist in bear hunting is the *quota hunt*. The California black bear hunting season, for example, is suspended once a preordained quota of animals has been killed. At press time, that quota was seventeen hundred bears. The state's black bear season ends when this quota is reached or on the last Sunday in December, whichever comes first. Checking with authorities daily as this quota is approached could save you a lot of grief later.

Some states suspend black bear seasons when a quota of bears or of sows is reached.

It is solely the hunter's responsibility to know if he or she has obtained the proper paperwork to hunt legally in a particular area. If paperwork is not correct, only the hunter will pay the price. Complete understanding of this one immutable fact before you begin to search for the perfect bear hunt is the only sure way to avoid a costly fine or, in the worst case scenario, suspension of hunting privileges.

Traveling to—or through—Canada becomes a real adventure when you must deal with Canada's firearms regulations (refer to Chapter 20 for more information). Remember that if you're driving to Alaska to hunt, you will have to travel through Canada. And don't forget that you must have the required paperwork from the U.S. Customs Department in order to bring your rifles back into the United States.

Example: Black Bear Hunting Restrictions in Alberta

As an example of the licensing requirements in just one of Canada's provinces, here are the nonresident alien (American and other non-Canadian nationalities) black bear hunting requirements for Alberta as we went to press. Requirements will change, of course, depending on where you plan to hunt or what bear species you plan to hunt.

- All nonresident aliens who want to hunt big game in Alberta are required by law to book their hunts with a registered Alberta outfitter.
- Archery hunters must obtain a separate Bowhunting Permit as well as all other Alberta licenses. The minimum bow draw poundage in this province is forty pounds, and broadheads must measure at least seven-eighths inch at their widest point.
- Crossbows are prohibited. A physically challenged hunter, however, who prequalifies for an exemption, may be awarded a special crossbow license.
- Firearms regulations are fairly liberal. Hunters may use either shotguns or rifles to bag their bears, within reason. It is unlawful to use:
- any ammunition less than .23 caliber and with an empty cartridge case less than 44 mm (1.75 inches) in length
- shotguns of .410 gauge or less
- ammunition loaded with nonexpanding bullets
- any auto-loader with the capacity to hold more than five cartridges in its magazine
- any fully automatic firearm, or any pistol, revolver or other firearm capable of firing more than one bullet during one pressure of the trigger

In addition, all Alberta hunters must possess a valid Wildlife Identification Number (WIN), and a Wildlife Certificate.

Current Alberta Non-Resident Licensing Fees are being provided for hunters who would like to estimate their costs prior to booking a hunt. All fees are expressed in Canadian dollars at the time we went to press. These fees do not include the seven percent Federal Goods and Service Tax or additional service charges. Each province may change its regulations and permit prices at any time, so do not assume that this information is totally accurate.

Always check before you book to be sure that no new regulations have been enacted or old ones changed.

EXAMPLE: BLACK BEAR HUNTING RESTRICTIONS IN ALASKA

To illustrate how much difference there is from one area to another, here are some of Alaska's restrictions:

In Alaska, hunters may generally possess and use firearms with few restrictions. State law prohibits the following firearms:

- fully automatic firearms
- rifles with barrels shorter than sixteen inches
- shotguns with barrels shorter than eighteen inches
- rifles or shotguns under twenty-six inches in total length.

Rifles, shotguns, and handguns are legal for hunting in Alaska. Rimfire cartridges generally may be used only for small game. See the Alaska Hunting Regulations for details.

Handguns may not be carried concealed except while a person is actually engaged in lawful hunting, trapping, fishing, or other lawful outdoor activity that "necessarily involves the carrying of a weapon for personal protection." This statutory exemption recognizes the need to protect firearms from rain or extreme cold.

Firearms carried in vehicles must be either in plain sight or, if concealed, out of reach of vehicle occupants. As a matter of safety, firearms being transported to or from the field must always be unloaded.

State law prohibits shooting on, from, or across a road. As a matter of safety and courtesy, hunters should not discharge firearms except when they're well away from roads.

Certain national park units have firearms restrictions. For current information about firearms use in these areas, contact Alaska Public Lands Information Centers.

Officials with Alaska's Department of Fish and Game require successful black bear hunters to obtain a seal from the closest fish and game office to legally transport harvested black bears. Those whose bear hunts are still in the planning stages should make it a point to check before departing with wildlife authorities in the state or province where they intend to hunt to verify whether similar restrictions or regulations are in effect.

Always thoroughly read wildlife regulations to determine what permits, licenses, and other paperwork you must have, and then talk to an outfitter to double-check your conclusions. After the two of you have agreed on paperwork and permitting requirements, including dates by which applications must be submitted, contact the

Always check the regulations before you book your hunt to make sure nothing goes wrong during your pursuit to a trophy. (Courtesy: Ted Rose)

provincial or state game department where you will be hunting. Confirm with them that your information is correct and that nothing else is needed to be in compliance with wildlife laws.

When planning your bear hunt, never take anything for granted. Be sure that when you tag the bear of a lifetime, nothing will go wrong to deprive you of your hard-earned trophy.

STAYING SAFE IN BEAR COUNTRY

No matter where you are hunting, always remember that each bear is an individual. You have no way of knowing, merely by observing a bear, what its life experiences are, nor can you determine whether it has had any previous experience with humans. This last point is particularly valid in backcountry areas. One bear may act just like another bear, or it may act like no other bear on the planet. Like people, bears are born with varying temperaments. Their moods often change from one day to the next or from one situation to another. A bear in poor physical condition is generally more dangerous than one in good condition, but nothing is engraved in stone when it comes to an assessment of bear attack probability.

Bears are the most dangerous game in North America and rank high on the list of the world's most dangerous game as well. Yet you are far more likely to be injured or killed in a traffic accident getting to bear camp than by a bear once you arrive. In 1990, statistics released by the National Safety Council revealed that forty-two thousand U.S. residents died in auto accidents, and about twenty-nine

You are far more likely to be injured or killed in a traffic accident getting to hunting camp than by a bear once you arrive. (Courtesy: M. R. James)

hundred drowned. Forty-one were killed by lightning, thirty-eight died from bee stings, twenty-four died from dog bites, and four died from bites by venomous snakes—but no one was killed by a bear.

Almost all bear attacks take place when people get too close to the animals, either on purpose or by accident.

Grizzly bears attack when surprised, when protecting their young, or when guarding their food. Black bears may become seriously annoyed and swat or cuff at an offender who may be too slow providing them with a handout or getting out of their way. Should a black bear do more than swat, nip, or cuff, it may be trying to make you its next meal.

Polar bears attack when protecting their young, but since these huge white animals are almost totally carnivorous, an attack is more likely the bear's way of selecting you as its next meal.

There is no "magic bullet" to arm yourself with before heading into bear country. In fact, the opposite may be true. Alaska, for example, will issue a citation to any hunter who shoots a bear that is trying to make off with the carcass or meat of an animal the hunter has recently taken. "No excuse," say officials of the state's Department of Fish and Game.

Likewise, hunters may get into serious trouble if they attempt to import U.S.-made bear spray into Canada. Canadian officials seem to have no problem with Canadian-manufactured sprays—but finding the American spray in a hunter's gear sets them off on the road to confiscation.

How can you stay safe in bear country? There are many sets of circumstances that should regulate your behavior in the backcountry. Here are a few pointers:

Before You Go into Bear Country

- Always tell someone where you are going and when you intend to return, and be sure it's someone who is familiar with the area in which you will be traveling. Good choices are game wardens, forest rangers, park rangers, BLM officials, and other agency officials, particularly any who are employed by nearby parks, wilderness areas, or other pertinent agencies. Leave a message with someone if these folks aren't available when you leave the area.
- If you're planning a do-it-yourself hunt, be sure to apply for the proper backcountry use permits well ahead of time.
- Never hike, hunt, or camp alone. It's safest to use bear country in groups.
- If you suspect that you are have trouble hearing in high-frequency ranges, see an ear specialist before heading into bear country. People who are unable to hear a bear foraging, whuffing, or popping its jaws nearby may be setting themselves up for disaster.

HIKING

- Always travel during daylight hours. Most bears move about near dawn or dusk.
- Use binoculars to scan the country ahead of you.
- Stick to open trails whenever possible.
- Never investigate the stench of rotting flesh. A bear may be lurking nearby to defend its kill.
- If you see ravens, magpies, or whiskey jacks swooping down on something or flying off at your approach, proceed cautiously. You may have discovered a bear's kill site.
- Consider wearing bear bells, talking, or singing to lessen your chances of surprising a bear. Discuss each of these tactics before engaging in them with your outfitter.
- Remain aware of wind direction. Wind blowing into your face or crosswise to you may not provide nearby bears with sufficient warning of your presence.
- Do not hike with a dog. An untrained dog may lead an angry bear back to you.
- Ride a horse only if you are an experienced rider. Inexperienced riders may be placed in greater danger if thrown by a horse made skittish by the presence of a bear.
- If you see a bear, do not try to move closer. Give all bears a wide berth.

CAMPING

- Set up camps away from trails. Bears use trails as travel lands.
- In forested areas, camp close to a good escape tree. Beware, though, that black bears can climb trees, and grizzlies will climb trees if strong branches provide a "ladder" up into the tree.
- Avoid camping close to bushes and shrubs.
- Avoid camping where bears like to travel, such as open stream banks or beaches.
- If possible, sleep in a tent.
- Never camp near bear sign.
- Never camp where you see evidence of an earlier dirty camp.
- Store sweet-smelling belongings or food at least a hundred yards from where you sleep. Hang provisions at least ten feet off the ground and four feet from any vertical support. String a line between the two trees and suspend your backpack from the line.
- If there are bear-proof platforms or bear poles, use them.
- Store excess food or garbage in well-sealed plastic bags, then lash the bags high up on a tree's trunk.
- If you're camping close to a vehicle, keep food in the vehicle's trunk. If you're in a campground, put the food in the storage locker provided by most campgrounds in bear country.

- Triangulate when camping in open country. In other words, pitch your tent in one location, move a hundred yards in another direction and store your provisions there, then move a hundred yards in another direction and cook there. The three points should form a triangle.
- Cook on stoves, not on open fires.
- Never cook in your tent.
- Avoid cooking smelly food like fish or bacon.
- If you cook in a tent in winter, when bears are rarely active, do not use that tent during seasons when bears are moving around actively. Food odors can adhere to fabrics such as canvas.
- Do not sleep in the same clothes you wore while cooking. Cache cooking clothes with your food stores.
- Whenever possible, stack gear between you and the wall of the tent.
- Use a flashlight when moving around after dark.
- If something grabs you while you are in your sleeping bag or tent, fight like hell. The bear has one thing in mind: eating you. You must fight it off.

DEALING WITH GARBAGE AND REFUSE

- Bring only what you will eat.
- Never bury garbage.
- If you burn garbage, be sure it is totally consumed by flames. If it is not, seal the refuse in plastic bags and pack it out.
- If you pack it in, pack it out. Garbage left behind could cost the next camper his or her life.
- Seal garbage in either two Ziploc plastic bags or a bear-proof container, and store it in your food cache.
- Dispose of used tampons in the same manner as garbage.
- Carry dishwater several hundred yards from camp before emptying it onto the ground to prevent food particles in the water from attracting bears.

HUNTING BIG GAME (OTHER THAN BEAR) IN BEAR COUNTRY

- Gut, pack, and remove the carcass as soon as possible.
- Immediately drag the carcass away from the gut pile.
- Never leave a gut pile or carcass near or on a trail.
- Try to leave carcasses farther than half a mile from trails or sleeping areas.
- Never drag a carcass back to camp. Instead, hang it out of reach of a bear— at least ten feet above the ground. Quarter the carcass, or cut it into smaller pieces if necessary.
- Always leave a carcass where you can see it from a distance and where you can approach it from upwind. Consider leaving an article of your clothing on the carcass (even if it is hanging) to discourage bears from visiting.

RETURNING TO A CARCASS IF YOU MUST LEAVE IT FOR AWHILE

- Observe the carcass and its vicinity with binoculars from a distance before you approach it.
- If the carcass has been moved or partially buried, be extremely cautious and alert to the presence of a bear.
- Remember that a bear may be bedded nearby. Make noise. Shout. Approach from upwind whenever possible.
- If a bear has claimed the carcass, leave it alone. Do not risk either your safety or the bear's.
- Report the incident to Fish and Game officials—whether the bear leaves, bluff-charges, or refuses to abandon a kill site.

BEAR SPRAY AND BEARS

It is a good idea to carry red pepper-based spray when traveling through bear country. This red pepper spray, the active agent of which is known as capsicum, is especially effective when used on black bears, younger brown bears or grizzlies, and grizzlies that are not guarding cubs or a kill site. But using the spray in other instances probably will not make a bad situation worse.

The bear's eyes should be your primary target when aiming pepper spray. Other aiming points include the animal's nose and mouth. If you spray at a bluff-charging bear when the animal is still several feet or more away, it will disperse before it can do any good. Spray into the bear's eyes, mouth, or nose when it approaches to within two feet or less. Some bear sprays are sold in chest or waist holsters

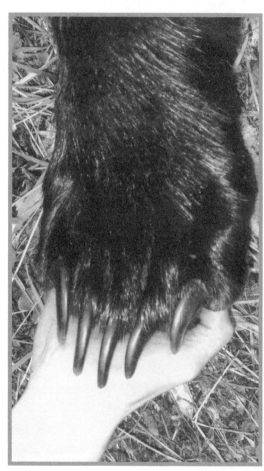

If an animal's carcass has been moved or partially buried in bear country, be extremely cautious whie approaching it. You don't want to get up close and personal with a griz and its lethal paws. (Courtesy: Jim Zumbo)

that make it easy to dispense the spray with a slight movement of the wearer's hand. Keeping the spray stream from affecting you can be a problem. Wind blowing from behind the bear and into your face could cause the spray to incapacitate you. If the wind is blowing crosswise, it may cause the spray to lose much of its punch as it drifts out of the bear's face.

Five ounces of bear spray is probably not enough. Opt instead for the nine-ounce size. You may need it.

If You See a Bear and You're Not Hunting

- Stand up as tall as possible and slowly wave your arms.
- Speak in a loud voice to let the bear know you are human.
- Always leave an escape route for a curious bear.
- Never, ever run, even if the bear bluff-charges.
- If the bear approaches, raise your voice. Be more aggressive. Bang pots and pans.

If a grizzly makes contact, surrender. Fall to the ground, roll into a ball, protect the back of your neck with your hands, and play dead. A grizzly will often break off its attack when the threat has been removed.

If the bear does not break off its attack, or if a black bear is attacking you, then fight back vigorously. Bite its nose, stick your fingers deep into its eyes, bite its ear, kick—do whatever it takes to get the animal off you.

If You Surprise a Bear

If you surprise a bear at close range and the animal starts woofing, huffing, hissing, popping or snapping its jaws, stomping its feet, lowering its head with its ears laid flat back, or staring directly at you, do not run. Back slowly away. Do not shout. Do not make any sudden movements. Avoid direct eye contact.

Outfitters and Lodges

California

Arrowhead Lodge
Clint Arrowsmith & Wes Arrowsmith
Red Bluff, CA 96080
Phone: 530-527-6419
Email: yogi@tehama.net

Maine

Cedar Ridge Outfitters
Hal & Debbie Blood
PO Box 744
Jackman, ME 04945
Phone: 207-668-4169
Email: blood@gwi.net
www.cedarridgeoutfitters.com

Gentle Ben's Lodge
Bruce Pelletier
Box 212 HP
Rockwood , ME 04478
Phone: 207-534-2201
Toll-free: 800-242-3769
Email: info@gentleben.com

New Mexico

Jason Turner
Gila Wilderness Outfitters
Phone: 505-538-9244
Toll-free: 888-884-2964

Wyoming

Scott Denny
Table Mountain Outfitters
PO Box 2714
Cheyenne, WY 82003
Phone: 307-632-6352
www.HuntingWyoming.Com

Quebec

George River Lodge
www.norpaq.com
Phone: 1-800-473-4650

Or contact Tourism Quebec
www.bonjour-quebec.com
Phone: 1-877-266-5687

Vancouver Island, B.C.

Jim Shockey
Pacific Rim Guide Outfitters
www.jimshockey.com
1-888-826-1011

BLACK BEARS, GRIZZLIES, BROWN BEARS, KODIAK BROWN BEARS, POLAR BEARS

ALASKA
Jim Bailey, Master Guide
P.O. Box 770695
Eagle River Alaska 99577
Phone: 907-696-2163
Fax: 907-696-2167
www.alaskaexperience.com

Thomas Kirstein
P.O. Box 83808
Fairbanks, AK 99708

Curly Warren
Stoney River Lodge
Phone: 907-696-2187
www.stoneyriver.com

BARREN GROUND GRIZZLIES

Jerome Knap
Canada North Outfitting
P.O. Box 3100
Ontario, Canada K0A 1A0
Phone: 613-256-4057
FAX: 613-256-4512
Email: cnonorth@istar.ca

Arctic North Guiding
Dennis Reiner
Phone: 907-457-6894
Email: dennis@arcticnorthguiding.com
Website: www.arcticnorthguiding.com

GRIZZLY BEARS

Chandalar River Outfitters
Keith C. Koontz
Phone: 907-451-6587
Email: kckoontz@alaska.net
Website: www.koontzAlaska.com

Phil Mancuso and his Eskimo guide and the result of a hunt arranged by Canada North Outfitters'
Jerome Knap. (Courtesy: Canada North Outfitters)

GRIZZLY AND BLACK BEARS; BOWHUNTING SPECIALTY

Bowron River Outfitters
Brett Thorpe
2773 Lonsdale St
Prince George, BC
Canada V2L 4W9
Phone: 250.612.0061
Email: brett@bowhuntingbc.com

GLACIER BEARS, GRIZZLIES, BLACK BEARS

Joe & Victoria Letarte
Box 16075
Two Rivers, Alaska 99716
Phone: 907-488-7517
Email: letarte@alaska.net

POLAR BEARS, BARREN GROUND GRIZZLY BEARS

Jerome Knap
Canada North Outfitting
P.O. Box 3100
Ontario, Canada K0A 1A0
Phone: 613-256-4057
FAX: 613-256-4512
Email: cnonorth@istar.ca

BOOKING AGENTS

Bob Lozinsky
WorldWide Wilderness
144 2nd Avenue North
Saskatoon, SK Canada S7K 2B2
Phone: 1-888-223-2117
Phone: 1-306-664-1616
Email: wilderness@wwwdi.com
www.wwwdi.com

Rich LaRocco
Associated Hunting Consultants
Phone: 435-752-7774
www.hunts.net

Bill Snodgrass Bear Hunts
Phone: 800-868-1119

FROM FIELD TO TABLE
ALL ABOUT BEAR MEAT

Remove all of the bear's scent glands when the animal is skinned. Do not allow the bear to hang for several days as some hunters do with deer. Aging a bear is not necessary and may actually encourage the growth of harmful organisms in the meat.

PREPARING BEAR MEAT

Bear is an excellent choice of meat, particularly when it is properly cared for, prepared, and cooked. Its texture is similar to that of pork, but the flavor can sometimes approach that of beef. The meat from younger bears can be cooked "as is," while the meat from older bears may be improved by marinating. A good marinade helps to tenderize bear meat and also removes much of its gamey taste.

The meat from a bear that has fed on carrion will not taste nearly as good as

If given proper field care, bear can be used as a substitute meat for many of your favorite recipes. (Courtesy: M. R. James)

that from an animal that has fed on berries or other sweet fruits. All visible fat, which has an extremely strong flavor, should be removed, along with other white matter such as sinews, veins, or lymph nodes. As bear meat cooks, baste it with butter or other shortening for best results. Taking time to properly prepare and cook bear meat will improve its taste.

Bears, like pigs, sometimes harbor trichinosis. To prevent possible contamination of anyone who eats bear meat, either store packages for a minimum of thirty days at −10°F or cook the meat until it reaches an internal temperature of 170°F.

Young bears are usually more tender than older animals. Young animals may be roasted, but don't overcook them. Moist methods of preparation work better when cooking meat from older bears. Consider marinating these cuts or using them in casseroles or stews.

If prepared properly in the field, bear can be used as a substitute meat in all of your favorite recipes. It works especially well as a substitute for venison or beef.

MEAT COMPARISON CHART

Species	Protein%	Fat%	Cholesterol(mg/100g*)
Bear (Black)	20.1	8.3	**
Beef (lean ground)	17.7	20.7	75
Beef (USDA Choice)	22.0	6.5	72
Buffalo	21.7	1.9	62
Caribou	22.6	3.4	67
Chicken	23.6	0.7	62
Deer (Mule)	23.7	1.3	107
Deer (Sitka)	21.5	2.7	18
Elk	22.8	0.9	67
Goose (Canada)	22.8	7.1	84
Grouse (Sharptail)	23.8	0.7	105
Mallard	23.1	2.0	140
Moose	22.1	0.5	71
Ptarmigan	24.8	2.3	20
Rabbit	21.8	2.3	81
Wigeon	22.6	2.1	131

* 100 grams = 31/2 ounces   ** Not available

ROAST BEAR IN RAISIN SAUCE

4-pound bear roast

2 $\frac{1}{2}$ cups water

1 cup red wine (a Chianti works well)

1 tablespoon flour

1 $\frac{1}{2}$ teaspoon dry mustard

$\frac{1}{2}$ teaspoon salt

$\frac{1}{4}$ teaspoon pepper

2 $\frac{1}{2}$ tablespoons lemon juice

$\frac{1}{2}$ cup seedless raisins

Remove all fat from the bear meat and place it in a roasting pan. Add two cups of the water and the wine and cover. Roast at 350°F for two and one-half hours.

Mix together the flour, dry mustard, salt, and pepper in a saucepan. Add the lemon juice and the remaining water and stir. Add the raisins. Cook slowly over medium heat, stirring constantly, until the mixture has the consistency of syrup.

Pour the raisin mixture over the bear roast and cover. Continue roasting for thirty minutes, basting with the raisin mixture three or four times during this time.

BEAR KABOBS

1 bottle Italian salad dressing (Wish Bone or Four Seasons
   work well)

dash of Worcestershire sauce

dash of low-salt soy sauce

salt and pepper

dash of Tabasco sauce (optional)

2 pounds bear meat cut into 1-inch chunks

cherry tomatoes

green peppers cut in squares

1 carton large mushrooms

onions, quartered

bacon (optional)

wooden or metal skewers (if wooden, soak them in water
   before using)

Pour the Italian dressing in a large glass or stainless steel bowl or container. Add the Worcestershire sauce, soy sauce, salt, and pepper. Add Tabasco sauce if you prefer spicier food. Add the meat and marinate in the refrigerator anywhere from three to four hours to twenty-four hours. Turn the meat every four to six hours if it's not completely covered by the dressing mixture.

Fire up the grill. While it's heating, fill the skewers: alternate meat on each skewer with a square of pepper, a chunk of onion, a cherry tomato, and a mushroom. If bear meat is too dry for your taste, wrap a piece of bacon around each chunk of meat before threading it on the skewer.

Place kebabs on the grill, cover with a sheet of aluminum foil, and let cook for several minutes, watching the flame for flares. Then turn them and use a soft brush to generously apply more marinade to meat and vegetables. Repeat several times.

Kebabs are done when tomatoes seem ready to fall off the skewers.

BEAR STEAKS ATHENA

2 pounds bear steaks sliced 1/2-inch thick and tenderized
    with a meat mallet
$\frac{1}{2}$ cup olive oil
1 glove garlic, minced
$\frac{1}{4}$ cup lemon juice
1 teaspoon salt
1 teaspoon pepper
$\frac{1}{2}$ teaspoon oregano
$\frac{1}{2}$ teaspoon marjoram
$\frac{1}{2}$ teaspoon rosemary
1 tablespoon olive oil (set aside)
$\frac{1}{2}$ cup ripe olives

Trim all visible fat from the bear meat before you tenderize it . Whisk together the olive oil, garlic, lemon juice, salt, pepper, oregano, marjoram, and rosemary. Pour this marinade into a suitably sized glass or stainless steel container, place the tenderized steaks into the marinade, and refrigerate for a minimum of two to three hours.

Grill, broil or sauté the steaks in the tablespoon of olive oil that was set aside. Cook on one side, turn over, add ripe olives to the pan, and cook thoroughly on the other side. Cook until the meat is well done.

Garnish the meat with the olive oil and olive mixture from the skillet, if any remains. Do not use the marinade to make gravy, as the bear meat may have given it a gamey flavor despite refrigeration.

BEAR 'N' BEANS

Bear: Take one to two pounds of bear meat from the animal's hindquarters or front shoulders. Cut it into chunks about two inches thick. Using about one-half ounce of Morton's smoke-flavored sugar cure or other ham-type cure for each pound of bear meat, rub the cure thoroughly into the bear meat, then place the meat in a glass or stainless steel container in the refrigerator for one to two weeks. The cure will keep the meat from going rancid.

When you are ready to prepare the rest of the recipe, remove the meat from the refrigerator. It will feel salty to the touch, so soak it for an hour in lukewarm water to remove this salty surface. If you have a smokehouse or charcoal smoker, you can place the meat in either and smoke it to the desired degree of smoky taste. Or you can add it to the beans immediately.

Beans
- 1 pound dry white navy beans
- 2 teaspoons dry mustard
- 3 medium onions, sliced or diced
- 1 tablespoon salt
- $^1/_2$ cup brown sugar
- $^1/_2$ cup molasses
- $^1/_4$ cup good quality barbecue sauce (KC Masterpiece Original works well)
- 2 tablespoons dill pickle juice or vinegar
- prepared bear meat

Soak the beans overnight. Drain and rinse. Cover them once more with water and stir in mustard, onions, salt, brown sugar, molasses, barbecue sauce, dill pickle juice and bear meat. Bake in the oven at 250°F with the lid firmly in place for six to eight hours.

Black bears yield some tasty and healthy game meat. (Courtesy: Ted Rose)

TROPHY BEAR STEAKS

This recipe is well suited for meat from those big old boars.

> 1 cup flour
> $1/2$ teaspoon salt
> $1/2$ teaspoon pepper
> $1/2$ teaspoon thyme
> 1 cup sliced onions
> 4 tablespoons bacon drippings
> bear steaks, sliced $1/2$-inch thick and then pounded with a meat mallet until paper thin
> 1 $1/2$ cups canned beef, chicken, or vegetable broth
> 1 cup red wine
> 2 tablespoons tomato paste

In a bowl, mix flour, salt, pepper, and thyme. After you pound the steaks thin, dredge them in the flour mixture and set them aside.

Sauté the onions in the bacon fat until well browned and transparent. Add the bear steaks and brown well on both sides. Add half of the wine and all the broth and bring to a boil. Cook briskly, stirring constantly, for five minutes. Turn the steaks, reduce the heat to a simmer, and cover the pan. Continue simmering for $1^1/2$ hours, checking occasionally to determine whether more liquid should be added.

Remove steaks to a platter. Add the tomato paste and any remaining wine to the pan juices. Stir. If you prefer a thicker sauce, stir together one cup of water and two teaspoons of flour in a cup and gradually pour into the pan drippings. Stir until smooth and thick. Adjust seasoning to taste, and serve over the steak.

HUCKLEBEARY BEAR

> 3 pounds bear steaks, sliced 1/2-inch thick
> 3 cloves garlic, crushed
> 1 orange or 1/4 cup orange juice
> 2 carrots, chopped
> 1 onion, chopped
> 2 bay leaves
> 1 teaspoon thyme

¹/₄ teaspoon allspice
1 teaspoon pepper
oil for browning
¹/₂ cup red wine
¹/₂ cup beef stock, canned beef broth, or consomme

Remove all visible fat from steaks and tenderize them with a meat mallet. Combine all ingredients in a glass or stainless steel container and let marinate in the refrigerator for a day. Turn or stir ingredients several times during the day.

Remove steaks from marinade. Brown in oil in a skillet over medium heat. Add the red wine and beef stock and stir. When well combined, transfer everything to a roasting pan and place it in the oven. Cook at 225°F for two to three hours.

Serve with Hucklebeary Sauce.

HUCKLEBEARY SAUCE

1 cup honey
2 tablespoons raspberry jam
¹/₂ cup red wine
1 cup huckleberries, blueberries, or raspberries
¹/₄ cup unsalted butter
1 teaspoon Chinese five-spice mix

Pour the honey into an ovenproof container and place it in the oven along with the bear meat, but do not add it to the meat yet. Cook until the honey has turned a rich, deep brown color.

Remove the honey from the oven. Cool it by adding the raspberry jam and the wine. When the bear meat is done, pour off the liquid from the meat pan and keep the meat warm while you finish the sauce. Strain it and add it to the honey mixture. Cook this mixture over medium heat until the liquid has been reduced to about two cups.

In a separate pan sauté the berries in the butter. Add the Chinese five-spice mix, and then add the berry mixture to the honey sauce.

Serve over bear meat. This recipe is excellent when served with German potato pancakes and a fresh green salad.

STATUS OF BEARS
THROUGHOUT THE WORLD

Most hunters are almost totally focused on the wildlife near their homes. Only a few become interested in the game animals of other regions, countries, or continents. Other people, mostly zoologists, biologists, naturalists, or SCI members, see the big picture. These people not only are interested in local or national wildlife species, but they also learn what they can about all the many species that inhabit the various regions and countries of the world. Many of these species, unfortunately, have fallen on tough times. For example, many bear species from places other than North America are generally in a state of decline. The sole exceptions are Asian brown bear populations and a few European brown bear populations. Even these bears, though, soon may run into trouble as human populations increase and development once more starts encroaching on critical habitats.

In China, the much-loved giant panda is extremely endangered. Pandas live in bamboo jungles at altitudes between six and fourteen thousand feet. The species is in decline because since the 1970s, panda habitat has shrunk by more than half. The Chinese have revered the panda, whom they call *beishung*—the white bear—for centuries. It is the panda's bad fortune, however, to be a native of a country where the human birth rate is high and wildlife conservation efforts are meager at best. When Theodore Roosevelt and his brother Kermit met with the Chinese in the 1920s, the Roosevelts remarked, "To the best of our judgment, he (the giant panda) . . . is to be found only in pockets, and is never abundant, even in these pockets."

The sloth bear and sun bear of southeast Asia are also in a serious state of decline although the animals still inhabit small, widely-scattered areas in India, Sri Lanka, and Bangladesh, some of which are now protected. Only Bhutan still provides the animals with a fairly substantial area in which to roam. At the opposite end of the spectrum very few sloth bears have been reported recently in Nepal, a country that was once inhabited by many of the animals.

The sun bear is in the most immediate danger of all the bears except for the giant panda because its rainforest habitat in southeast Asia is rapidly disappearing. These seriously threatened animals are now found in Southeast Asia, from Burma eastward to Laos, Thailand, Cambodia, Viet Nam, Malaysia. Sun bears are also found on the islands of Sumatra and Borneo in the countries of Indonesia, Malaysia, and Brunei. Persistent reports of sun bear sightings continue to come from China, particularly in Yunan province. Whether sun bears still exist in Bangladesh is highly questionable, while it is likely that the animals are now extinct in India.

The IUCN (World Conservation Union) has classified as "vulnerable" the Asiatic black bear, an animal that once ranged over large parts of central and eastern Asia. The current status of this species is unknown in many portions of its range.

Habitat loss, as well as mortality caused by those who kill the sloth, sun, and Asiatic bears for their gallbladders, paws, and bile, seems to be increasing. Both factors are proving devastating to these bears. As habitat disappears, only a fragmented patchwork of jungle remains. There the small bear populations grow ever more isolated as well as genetically at risk from inbreeding.

The Asiatic black bear's distant South American cousin, the spectacled bear, is also known as *oso de anteojos, yanapuma,* or black puma. The Incas captured spectacled bears during organized predator roundups to protect their domestic anmals, but they usually set the bears free again because they believed the bears' spirits were responsible for making sick people well and also for guiding the souls of the dead into heaven.

Spectacled bears are the only bears found exclusively south of the equator. They are also hunted for their bile and parts. Spectacled bears seem to be doing the best in Ecuador's mountain cloud forests, portions of Peru, and parts of Bolivia. They can be found in Peru's coastal deserts at an altitude of just seven hundred feet as well as just below the permanent snowline at about fourteen thousand feet in Peru's Andes mountains. Spectacled bears can also be found in the steppe country, grassland habitats, and *paramos,* which can be best described as high altitude islands in a sea of forest.

Authorities with the IUCN believe that slightly more than eighteen thousand spectacled bears survive in the wild in the three Andes mountain ranges that encompass portions of Venezuela and extend to the border between Argentina and Bolivia. This estimate may be far off, though, and its margin of error could mean that there are several times the estimated eighteen thousand spectacled bears living in the wild.

In Europe, brown bear numbers are increasing in Sweden, Slovakia, and possibly European portions of Russia. The populations are stable in Finland, Estonia, Poland, Croatia, Slovenia, and probably Albania. Decreasing numbers of bears inhabit Romania, Ukraine, Bosnia, the Yugoslav Federation, and Bulgaria. The brown bear populations of Norway, Latvia, the Czech Republic, Greece, Macedonia, Austria, Italy, Spain, and France are threatened or endangered. There is no reliable information on brown bear status in Belarus or Turkey.

Polar bear numbers are stable or increasing in Canada, Norway, Greenland, Russia, and the United States.

North American brown bear populations are stable or increasing in both Canada and in the United States. One organization says that the prairie population of grizzly bears in Canada has been extirpated, although Alberta bear biologists report that four hundred of the animals are living in a refuge in the eastern part of the province.

THREAT TO BEARS

Throughout history, bears have been threatened mainly by humankind and other large predators. Short-faced bears probably preyed on less aggressive bear species such as the American black bear. Saber-toothed tigers undoubtedly took their share of bears, as did other large carnivores that roamed the earth during prehistoric times.

Bears, however, wherever they were found, were able to fight back or overcome obstacles to survive in good numbers until relatively recently.

The outcome has been mixed in North America. Bears as a whole are doing better here than in most other places. The American black bear in particular has moved into portions of its historic range that were unoccupied for many years, and the overall population is probably higher now, at just under one million individuals, than at any other time in history. Grizzly numbers in the lower forty-eight states continue to rebound, andn polar bear numbers are also increasing. Brown bear and grizzly numbers in Canada and Alaska seem to be increasing as well, but continued attempts to discredit those who believe populations are increasing by those in favor of protecting all brown bears in North America has muddied the waters to such an extent that it is difficult to know for certain where brown bear numbers stand.

One statistic that seems irrefutable is that the size of the average brown bear now being taken is smaller than it once was. Although many good-sized Kodiak and Alaska brown bears continue to be harvested by hunters, rarely is a specimen taken that compares in skull size or age to some of the animals taken just after World War

Polar bears are doing well in almost every portion of their range. Here sled dogs bring a giant boar to bay. (Courtesy: Canada North Outfitting)

II, when interest in hunting these bears first became apparent. There may be more brown bears in these areas, but they aren't attaining the extreme size that earlier generations of bears did.

Quite a hue and din accompanies any discussion about North American bears, with hunting opponents quite vocal about the "irreparable harm" being done to these species. The opposite appears to be true. North American bears are in either excellent shape or satisfactory shape or doing reasonably well in all parts of their range, despite hunting pressure.

Such is not the case in other areas of the world, where some brown bear populations are in imminent danger of extinction unless immediate attempts are made by bear protectionists to purchase critical habitat or relocate bears from other places to add a new genetic component to bloodlines compromised by generations of inbreeding.

In some areas of Europe and Asia, brown bears are increasing their range and could be said to be doing well—if people would leave the animals alone. Unfortunately, in some areas people have become used to not having to deal with bears, so when bears start raiding their oat fields, apple orchards, or beehives, the people immediately kill the nuisance animals, which is a blow to recovering populations. The bears are killed legally, but such killings are a real threat to the population if the rate of killing becomes too high or if the local bear population is small. Bear protectionists should probably make an effort to reimburse farmers and other locals for economic losses caused by bears in much the same way that a group called Defenders of the Wildlife is paying ranchers for wolf predation near Yellowstone Park. Once the bear population grows large enough to sustain some hunting pressure, hunting should be allowed. This would place a value on the bears, and hunting income would boost the local economy.

Poaching remains a threat to many, but not all bears. Populations subjected to widespread poaching are difficult to manage since poachers don't differentiate between taking a boar, a sow, or cubs. Bears in areas with widespread economic and social problems, such as Albania, Bulgaria, Bosnia, and the Yugoslav Federation, are under constant pressure from poachers.

Adult brown bear females with cubs are culled in many areas of eastern Europe and Asia to obtain cubs for circus acts or street performances. Dancing bears are fairly common in these countries, but they're rare where there is an economic incentive to protect bears for future economic benefit through hunting.

As long as wolves kill domestic herds and wild boars decimate small green gardens, especially in Europe and Asia, people will retaliate by setting traps for these creatures. Bears, of course, may also be guilty of predation and crop destruction. Nevertheless, when farmers on small farms set snares for wild boars or put out poison earmarked for problem wolves, bears too are killed. The bear populations in Spain have suffered severe mortality due to measures like these.

ILLEGAL TRADE IN BEAR PARTS

Bear parts have been used in traditional medicine in most parts of the world for about five thousand years. The first recorded prescription calling for the use of a bear's gallbladder as medicine was dated during the seventh century. Gallbladders and bile are important products in the illicit trade in bear parts which continues even today.

Bears have been regarded with awe by people since the dawn of time. Their great strength, their resemblance to humans, and their solicitous behavior toward their young were all regarded as admirable traits by primitive peoples. That admiration continues to the present time as people look to the bear—an animal that personifies rising from the dead in its ability to go underground and exist on nothing for several months and then emerge in the spring—to cure what ails them. Bear claws, paws, and teeth are in high demand for use in ceremonies and to wear as amulets to ward off evil spirits. Bear paws are also sold as a delicacy in certain parts of the world. These traditional uses of bear

Bear paws – like these from Bob Fromme's huge Kodiak brown – are sold as a delicacy in certain parts of the world and this contributes to declining populations of some bears.

parts have their origins far back in time. Education of the offending people may help to diminish trade in bear parts, but education alone will probably not be enough to eliminate it for many generations to come.

An increased demand for bear parts, especially bile, has led to a tremendous increase in poaching in Russia. The fall of communism in the Soviet state has had a terrible impact on the average Russian's ability to provide for his or her family. Bears are fairly numerous in some areas of Russia, and since Russia's trade in bear parts is mostly with nearby Asian countries like South Korea and China, it is fairly easy for Russians to continue in this illicit business with no negative ramifications.

The primary product driving the trade in bear parts is gallbladders. Bear galls contain a bile enzyme called *ursodeoxycholic acid,* or UDCA, which is thought by some Asian cultures to have medicinal and aphrodisiac properties. UDCA is being synthetically produced—and has been for many years—but some people refuse to use it even though it can be bought legally. The synthetic is an exact duplicate of real bile, but as long as folks still experience rapture when they consider the bear and its great spirit, it's no wonder that the mysticism inherent in an animal that was a living, breathing wild creature increases the demand for real bile. This kind of thinking means that even today, in parts of Asia bear bile sells for more money per gram than either cocaine or gold.

The use of bear parts, as well as the continuing trade in such items, is directly responsible for the decline of many of the world's bear species, including Asiatic black bears, sun bears, and sloth bears. The bear-part trade affects North American bears as well, because those who use bear parts do not really care where the parts come from as long as they belonged to a bear. British Columbia's Ministry of the Environment, Wildlife Branch, estimates that one bear may be killed illegally in the province for every bear that is killed legally. This is very disturbing, but equally disturbing is the fact that at a recent symposium on bears, authorities revealed statistics that seem to support their contentions that more than half the demand for bear bile within British Columbia comes from people who live there.

Although CITES (Convention on the International Trade in Endangered Species) continues to prohibit trade in all eight species of bear internationally, the regulation and enforcement of this prohibition is extremely difficult, and that is why many agencies now require that hunters check in all bears legally taken so that they can remove the bears' gallbladders. By thus eliminating the supply of legal galls, officials hope to shut down the legal trade in bear parts and thereby impede the sale of illegal parts. Unfortunately, as long as it is legal to trade in the parts of a bear taken legally by hunters, the illegal trade will continue to flourish.

In Russia, hope for the future may be found in the country's still-untapped brown bear hunting possibilities. As hunters learn about the wonderful brown bear hunting available there, the economic law of supply and demand may be brought to bear upon to poachers who deal in bear parts. Locals who make a living as hunting guides may be able to help weed out the poachers, who endanger the entire population for a few bear parts. As Russia stabilizes, adequate law enforcement with a mandate to protect bears should also eventually make a difference.

OTHER THREATS

As for North America, although brown bears as a whole are doing reasonably well, troubling trends are developing on the environmental horizon. Some coastal brown bear populations have been placed at risk due to an increased schedule of logging activity within British Columbia. Out of 353 British Columbian coastal valleys, only seventy remain in their once-pristine condition, and unfortunately, fifty-five of these are slated to be logged soon. When logging begins, roads will be built into these formerly roadless wilderness tracts. When hunters are able to access formerly hidden grizzly haunts by vehicle, the entire bear population will experience a severe decline, at least over the short term. Poachers as well as hunters will gain access to these areas. The bears will be the losers, and so will hunters when the number of available bear permits plummets for future seasons.

Salmon stocks are also in decline. In British Columbia alone, 142 known stocks of salmon have gone extinct, and 642 additional stocks are considered to be at high risk of extinction. Bears, particularly coastal browns and grizzlies, make a good portion of their livelihoods catching salmon. As stocks decline, so will reproductive rates, and bear density numbers will further decrease. This is serious—and bad—news for those who gaze upon brown bears as the symbol of the vanishing North American wilderness.

Development too is taking its toll. As humans flock to build cabins and homes near national and provincial parks, grizzly habitat becomes fragmented and then isolated. The latest estimate from Parks Canada stated that there are only about two hundred grizzly bears remaining in all of Canada's national parks in the northern Rockies, despite the fact that the parks are located in the heart of prime grizzly habitat.

Above the Arctic Circle, polar bear numbers continue to increase slowly, although with many more male bears within the Alaskan population there is evidence that cub mortality is rising, too. Whether continued stringent hunting regulations are good or bad for the species as a whole

What effect global warming may have on polar bears no one knows. Here are the tracks and scat of one of these huge white bears—and a hunter's glove. (Courtesy: Canada North Outfitting)

is a matter of much debate. Individual bears may be growing larger, but cub survival rates are lower than they could be were there additional hunting opportunities. Additional hunting would remove some of the larger male bears that prey on cubs. (There is a method to the male polar bear's cub-killing madness: With cubs no longer at her side, a female will enter estrus and the male will be able to breed with her again.)

Polar bears are at risk from persistent organic pollutants such as polychlorinated biphenyls (PCBs) and chlordanes that build up in the blubber of marine mammals like the ringed seal, the polar bear's primary food source. Norwegian scientists in 1997 found several hermaphroditic polar bear cubs with high levels of PCBs in their systems. Also of concern are the effects of nuclear radiation emitted by waste jettisoned from nuclear submarines beneath the polar ice cap. The Arctic has historically been such a pristine environment that no one is yet sure what increases in contaminant levels will mean to animals like polar bears that have never before been subjected to contaminants.

Global warming could continue into the future, resulting in the loss of glaciers as well as gradual melting of even more areas of the polar ice cap. What effect this will have on polar bears is not certain.

The threats to bears of all species remain troubling to people who care about the future of these magnificent creatures. The best weapon for fighting these some-times troubling trends is a thorough understanding of the problems involved as well as a mind open to all possible solutions.

INSTRUCTIONS FOR MEASURING BEAR

Measurements are taken with calipers or by using parallel perpendiculars, to the nearest **one-sixteenth** of an inch, without reduction of fractions. Official measurements cannot be taken until the skull has air dried for at least 60 days after the animal was killed. All adhering flesh, membrane and cartilage must be completely removed **before** official measurements are taken.

A. Greatest Length is measured between perpendiculars parallel to the long axis of the skull, without the lower jaw and excluding malformations.

B. Greatest Width is measured between perpendiculars at right angles to the long axis.

ENTRY AFFIDAVIT FOR ALL HUNTER-TAKEN TROPHIES

For the purpose of entry into the Boone and Crockett Club's® records, North American big game harvested by the use of the following methods or under the following conditions are ineligible:

I. Spotting or herding game from the air, followed by landing in its vicinity for the purpose of pursuit and shooting;
II. Herding or chasing with the aid of any motorized equipment;
III. Use of electronic communication devices, artificial lighting, or electronic light intensifying devices;
IV. Confined by artificial barriers, including escape-proof fenced enclosures;
V. Transplanted for the purpose of commercial shooting;
VI. By the use of traps or pharmaceuticals;
VII. While swimming, helpless in deep snow, or helpless in any other natural or artificial medium;
VIII. On another hunter's license;
IX. Not in full compliance with the game laws or regulations of the federal government or of any state, province, territory, or tribal council on reservations or tribal lands;

Please answer the following questions:

Were dogs used in conjunction with the pursuit and harvest of this animal?
☐ **Yes** ☐ **No**

If the answer to the above question is yes, answer the following statements:

1. I was present on the hunt at the times the dogs were released to pursue this animal.
☐ **True** ☐ **False**

2. If electronic collars were attached to any of the dogs, receivers were not used to harvest this animal.
☐ **True** ☐ **False**

To the best of my knowledge the answers to the above statements are true. If the answer to either #1 or #2 above is false, please explain on a separate sheet.

I certify that the trophy scored on this chart was not taken in violation of the conditions listed above. In signing this statement, I understand that if the information provided on this entry is found to be misrepresented or fraudulent in any respect, it will not be accepted into the Awards Program and 1) all of my prior entries are subject to deletion from future editions of **Records of North American Big Game** 2) future entries may not be accepted.

FAIR CHASE, as defined by the Boone and Crockett Club®, is the ethical, sportsmanlike and lawful pursuit and taking of any free-ranging wild, native North American big game animal in a manner that does not give the hunter an improper advantage over such game animals.

The Boone and Crockett Club® may exclude the entry of any animal that it deems to have been taken in an unethical manner or under conditions deemed inappropriate by the Club.

Date:_____ Signature of Hunter:_____
(SIGNATURE MUST BE WITNESSED BY AN OFFICIAL MEASURER OR A NOTARY PUBLIC.)

Date:_____ Signature of Notary or Official Measurer:_____

Score chart for bear reprinted courtesy of the Boone and Crockett Club,
250 Station Dr., Missoula, MT 59801
(406)542-1888, www.boone-crockett.org

APPENDIX

Records of
North American
Big Game

250 Station Drive
Missoula, MT 59801
(406) 542-1888

BOONE AND CROCKETT CLUB®

OFFICIAL SCORING SYSTEM FOR NORTH AMERICAN BIG GAME TROPHIES

BEAR

	MINIMUM SCORES		KIND OF BEAR (check one)
	AWARDS	ALL-TIME	
black bear	20	21	☐ black bear
grizzly bear	23	24	☐ grizzly
Alaska brown bear	26	28	☐ Alaska brown bear
polar bear	27	27	☐ polar

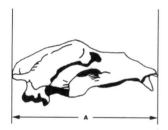
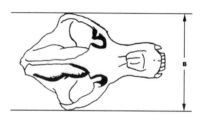

SEE OTHER SIDE FOR INSTRUCTIONS	MEASUREMENTS
A. Greatest Length Without Lower Jaw	
B. Greatest Width	
FINAL SCORE	

Exact Locality Where Killed:

Date Killed: Hunter:

Owner: Telephone #:

Owner's Address:

Guide's Name and Address:

Remarks: (Mention Any Abnormalities or Unique Qualities)

I, _____ , certify that I have measured this trophy on _____
    PRINT NAME   MM/DD/YYYYY

at _____
  STREET ADDRESS   CITY   STATE/PROVINCE

and that these measurements and data are, to the best of my knowledge and belief, made in accordance with the instructions given.

Witness: _____ Signature: _____ I.D. Number ☐☐☐☐
     B&C OFFICIAL MEASURER